THE GATE OF GATES

Moath Alofi
Philippe Cardinal

THE
GATE OF
GATES

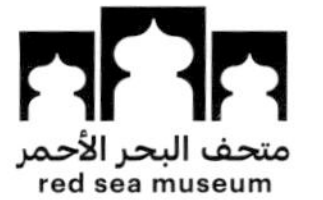

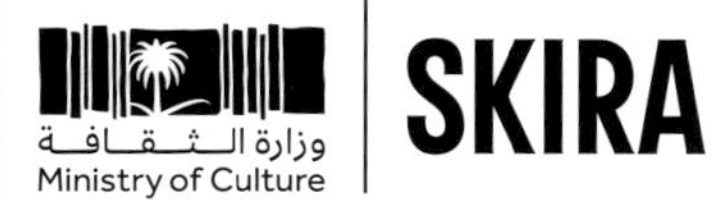

SKIRA

The exhibition *The Gate of Gates*
is presented at the Red Sea Museum,
inaugurated in 2025 by the Museums
Commission, Ministry of Culture,
Saudi Arabia.

**His Highness Prince Badr bin Abdullah
bin Mohammed bin Farhan Al Saud**
Minister of Culture

**His Excellency Hamed bin
Mohammed Fayez**
Vice Minister of Culture

Artist
Moath Alofi

Curator
Philippe Cardinal

Scenography
Nathalie Crinière, Matteo Soyer,
Maëlys Chevillot

Design and Supervision
Anne Jaffrennou, Anne Frese,
Tiphaine Massari, Habib Ghaziri,
Bahaa Hassoun

Lighting Design
François Roupinian,
Maricar Bustamante, Erika Solorzano

Production
Samer El Bizri, Milio Ghanem,
Lee Bodington, Mazin Rahal

Printing
Raquel Ramos, Laurent Poingt

Framing
Victor Guedes, José Rocha

Installation
Marina Lagos, Ece Gunay

Logistics and Shipping
Philippe da Silva, Philippe Bienvenu,
Jérémie Margitay, Marie Poivret

Conservation
Jorge Mamede, Vânia Assis,
Carolina Ventura

RED SEA MUSEUM

Eman Zidan
Director

Doha Abouelenien
Collection Management

Geraldine Hebras, Yussor Alkhateeb
Exhibitions and Programs

MUSEUMS COMMISSION

Mona Khazindar
Chief Executive Officer

Ibrahim Alsanousi
*General Manager, Museums
and Concept Development*

Dr. Sylvain Fort
*General Manager, Museums
and Assets*

Dr. Jana Jabbour
Director of Communication

Hagar Adam
*Publications Department Senior
Specialist*

Dr. Virginia Cassola
Curatorial Collections Director

Nizar Ibrahim
*Architectural Design and Planning
Manager*

Salwa Samargandi
Architectural Design Team Lead

Abdullah AlShareef
Shared Services Project Manager

Hanin Saber
Shared Services Senior Specialist

Essa Alkhaldi
Project Management Office Director

Hussein Al Abbad
*Logistics and Operations Services
Manager*

Abdullah Alfaifi
*Logistics and Operations Senior
Specialist*

Abdulaziz Badawi
Facility Management Manager

Contents

Preface

Heritage buildings often have a significance that goes beyond their historical value. They have a soul and a memory that transcend the materiality of their physical space. No place better illustrates this transcendence as Bab al-Bunt in the heart of the Kingdom of Saudi Arabia.

Located in Jeddah's historic downtown district al-Balad, which was recognized as a UNESCO World Heritage Site in 2014, Bab al-Bunt is a magnificent heritage building with a unique aesthetic, architectural, cultural, and historical significance. For decades, it represented the main gateway through the Red Sea for millions of Muslim believers from around the world who traveled to Holy Mecca to perform their pilgrimage, turning Jeddah into the gateway to Mecca. It is in this building overlooking the sea that they were held in quarantine and provided with health services before being transferred to their cherished destination – Mecca.

In line with its efforts to preserve cultural heritage and celebrate national identity, the Ministry of Culture of the Kingdom of Saudi Arabia has endowed Bab al-Bunt with a cultural vocation. We have repurposed the hundred-year-old heritage building into the Red Sea Museum, a new cultural and artistic destination that provides an extraordinary insight into the history of human interactions and cross-cultural encounters that have shaped the Red Sea.

Through the Red Sea Museum's inaugural exhibit *The Gate of Gates*, we have taken on the ambitious mission of bringing life back to a heritage building by capturing its soul and reviving its memory. By commissioning Saudi internationally renowned artist Moath Alofi to photograph Bab al-Bunt prior to its renovation and repurposing as a museum, we aimed to encapsulate the sense of this iconic place, rich in history and memory. The result is a unique corpus of photographs that magically uncover the spirit of Bab al-Bunt by powerfully conveying the aspirations, memories, dreams, and feelings of pilgrims, merchants, and dwellers who have turned Bab al-Bunt into the "Gate of Gates."

This exhibition, like other temporary exhibitions that will be held at the Red Sea Museum, contributes to the Ministry of Culture's ambition to promote culture as a way of life, by enabling the public to explore new horizons, experiment with new art approaches, and engage with the museum. We hope, through this exhibition, to provide Saudi and international visitors with the unique opportunity to travel through time and space to discover an architectural and historical jewel closely tied to our cultural heritage.

HH Prince Badr bin Abdullah bin Farhan Al Saud
Minister of Culture

The Gate of Gates

Philippe Cardinal

THE SPACES OF AL-BUNT

When Moath Alofi entered the building of Bab al-Bunt, it was empty. Originally built by the sea, designed as the Sanitary Office for welcoming pilgrims disembarking at Jeddah, it has now been decades that the site no longer serves this purpose, decades as well that the sea no longer comes to lap at the walls.

The edifice was empty or, more precisely, it had been emptied of everything that had been abandoned by the successive administrations that had used its rooms over the years, transforming some into offices, others into warehouses and sheds. This emptiness was a very temporary state of affairs, as the photographer knew. Renovation work was to be undertaken to transform Bab al-Bunt into the Red Sea Museum.

It was in this brief hiatus, then, and in this void, that Moath Alofi intervened. A void that this son of Madi-nah had nothing to fear, since he is used to frequenting the desert. Yet a kind of vertigo might have seized the visitor, as though he perceived – beyond years, decades, centuries, and even an entire millennium – the almost tangible presence, in this precise location, of thousands, tens and hundreds of thousands, millions and tens of millions of other visitors, all pilgrims, new arrivals, wear-ing immaculate *ihram* and preparing to accomplish the first terrestrial steps of their pilgrimage on the soil of the Hejaz.

When Moath Alofi walked into Bab al-Bunt to photograph the building, he was unaware of nearly ev-erything about the chronology of its construction, simply because nobody knows this exactly. The edifice that the photographer had before his eyes was the result of vari-ous successive architectural acts and interventions over time, which had been undertaken by different architects and construction crews, about whom we no longer know anything today.

The building – as it was constructed in the late nineteenth or early twentieth century – contained only one level. It was separated from the sea only by a sim-ple awning made of palm leaves, designed to shelter the pilgrims upon their arrival. The edifice was later rearranged and expanded. In the 1930s or 1940s, it was notably endowed with an upper storey and two semi-cir-cular wings. A series of solid archways constituting a canopy formed an improvement to replace the palm-leaf awning; its prominence on the coast largely surpassed that of the edifice, to create a vast landing area. The final version of this canopy – mounted several years prior to the erection of the building's new floor – contained over twenty arches, in very weakly reinforced concrete, whose construction thus derived from a very recent technological innovation. After the reconfiguration of the port, in the 1970s, Bab al-Bunt was deprived of its access to the sea and the canopy was partly demolished. Only seven of its arches subsist to this day.

Other modifications, mainly internal, also took place over the years. The most recent among these, post-2000s, saw a good deal of the walls taken down to enlarge certain spaces, within the framework of a renovation project that was never completed.

Moath Alofi, as we mentioned, entered Bab al-Bunt before the building was delivered to those whose task consisted of transforming the site into the Red Sea Museum. The edifice was empty, we also said. The pho-tographer was to latch onto this void – not systemati-cally, however, but at least initially. This vacancy was simply present there and stood out to him, without dic-tating the approach he should follow.

The photographer would then present what we can qualify as an initial set of images, strictly dedicated to the arrangement of the various architectural elements and the layout of the spaces as he discovered them at the time of his visit. What is striking about these pho-tographs is the homogeneity and coherence emanating from them, which is all the more surprising in that the current Bab al-Bunt building is the product of a long series of interventions and modifications that have taken place over time and that ought to have conferred to the edifice, as we might expect, a clearly more composite appearance. This singularly paradoxical coherence, this harmony – emanating from the series of photographs that Moath Alofi devotes to the description of al-Bunt's spaces – aligns with the sense of plenitude that all of these men must have shared, over time, and whose presence there had been a guarantee of accomplishment.

What can be captured in these images is the power of certainty, shared by all those who, coming from far, far away – sometimes the ends of the world – reached this place after a journey combined with a spiritual undertaking that was most often a once-in-a-lifetime occurrence. It is precisely there, in this spot, installed on the shore, on the western flank of the city, prior to the wall that surrounds it, that would land those, among the pilgrims, who had not chosen to take the long terrestrial routes that the caravans took, but had rather entrusted their fate to the ships that converged on Jeddah from all over, braving the winds and waves of the seas and oceans.

We know that the conditions of these journeys were, for centuries and centuries, extremely difficult and exhausting. A lot of these boats were shipwrecked, notably in the Red Sea, which was particularly difficult to navigate. With the relief of having escaped grave perils, the pilgrims would set foot on terra firma, filled with joy and the certainty of having now attained their goal, having their feet on the Hejaz soil, with only one day's walk separating them from the city of Mecca. They knew that they were on the eve of crossing the very last segment of an immense journey, undertaken for weeks, months, sometimes even years, giving rise in them to a feeling of accomplishment coupled with rapture, a euphoria that would not leave them.

Some of this bliss can be seen in Moath Alofi's images of al-Bunt. However, behind this edifice, a plethora of others implicitly appear. The current building was naturally preceded by another – erected in the years after the completion of the Suez Canal (1869) – which appears rather indistinctly on a few old photographs of the city of Jeddah. Further back in time, travelers from the early nineteenth century evoked the presence of a similar building, still in this same location. A "Sanitary Office," as it was indicated on its pediment in the early twentieth century; or "Quarantine," as it was designated in the latter half of the nineteenth century; or simply the "Custom House": the building is still situated there, ahead of the city walls, irrespective of the terms used to refer to it. Creating one of the oldest known maps of the city of Jeddah, after his brief visit there in 1762, en

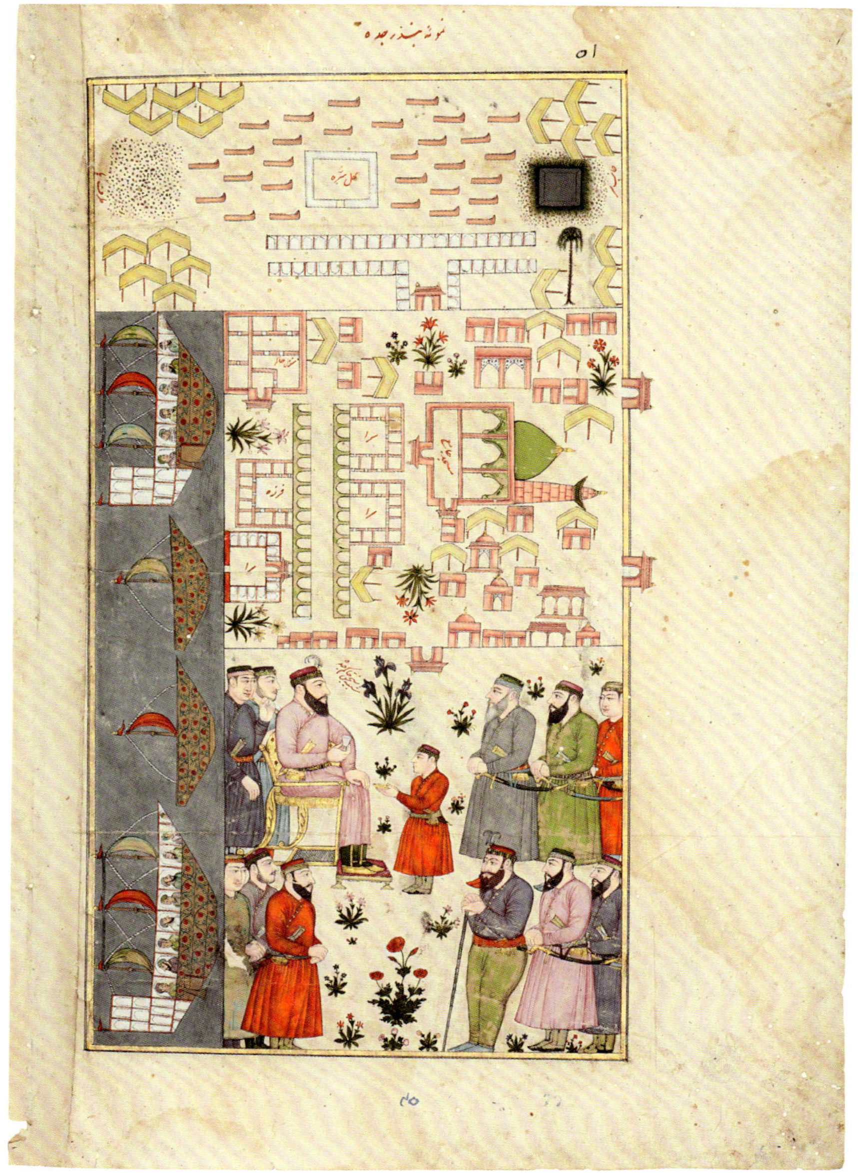

route for Yemen, the famous Danish traveler Carsten Niebuhr used the name Custom House to indicate on his map the presence of such a building, still in this same place. Another century earlier, circa 1677, the Indian Safi ibn Vali, with his artist's soul, had made a precious ink, watercolor, and gold leaf illustration of Jeddah, on which we can recognize an early ancestor of this building, by the sea, where pilgrims from all over the world landed.

Further back, we lack testimonies and documents to illustrate or even evoke the former states of this building. One thing, however, is certain: it has indeed always been there that the pilgrims have landed, since the origins, or rather, since AH 26, when, according to the tradition, the Caliph Uthman chose Jeddah as the port of Mecca. It is there that, ever since that date, a structure has always existed to welcome these travelers driven by the purest of aspirations. Something of this purity emerges in the photographs that Moath Alofi offers of the Bab al-Bunt building. A serenity emanates from these images that may first appear cold, almost glacial, but an intense vibration wells up as we consider them. The power of these photographs may well reside therein. A timeless dimension also emanates from them, as though the plethora of buildings and landing platforms built on this site over the centuries could be glimpsed in the photographer's images. As though, by photographing al-Bunt's spaces, Moath Alofi managed to allow the building to exist across time and space.

THE IRON GATES

The elegant sobriety with which these photographs have been designed and the wholly empathetic restraint with which the photographer broached his subject clearly have something to do with the success of his project. What is also striking about the photographer's approach is his refusal of an aesthetically pleasing temptation that would mislead the viewer. Moath Alofi strives to show the building as it really is – in other words, as it appears at the time of the visits that he pays to it.

The first of the photographer's tasks consisted, as we mentioned, in taking stock of the building's spatial organization. Next, he engages in a rather strange inventory. Careful not to install a hierarchy among the themes of the images that he creates along the way, the photographer allows himself to be guided by the building much more than he submits it to an interpretation of his own. He is thus able to subjugate his point of view to that commanded by the places, assisted in this, perhaps, by the temporal suspense in which the building finds itself – it has not been a Sanitary Office or a Custom House for decades, but is not yet a museum. Moath Alofi was well aware that he was operating within this interval, which enabled him to apprehend Bab al-Bunt in a moment of stripping, of laying bare.

So, the photographer manages to place himself now and then in a mood whereby he lets the building dictate the images he should take. It was in this way that he was able to create a series of photographs presenting openings piercing the walls of the edifice, usually arranged in sequence, held by metal beams and girders. The walls of the edifice are demolished, with iron clasping them, and at first seem to attest to some of the destructive forces exerted against them. We can therefore guess the reticence with which the author of these photographs has adopted this subject, concerning

which – as if reluctant – he later returns many times and whose cold intensity he eventually appropriates. It is not at all a demolition enterprise that the photographs of Moath Alofi attest to in this instance, but something altogether different, since he was able to identify, between the flanks of the building, the presence of a singular allegory.

We clearly understand, when considering these images, that the very fabric of the edifice has been violated. The tearing down of these walls – built with coral stones, emblematic of Jeddah's architecture for centuries – has disturbed a former state of the building. Despite the fact that they were created recently, these gaping holes – and, therefore, Moath Alofi's photographs of them – nevertheless reflect a permanence that we could describe, once again, as timeless.

That is why they are so striking. And the credit goes to the photographer for having detected their evocative power. These openings – framed by metal beams and braces, which make them appear clenched within steel jaws – cannot be confused with doors, with which the building is also abundantly endowed. Their size and grandeur equally disqualify this, as does the fact that they are equipped with neither swing nor stable doors. Or, if these are doors, they are of the utterly allegorical variety. Gateway to Jeddah. Gateway to Hejaz. Gateway to Arabia. Gateway to Pilgrimage. This is precisely what these photographs might suggest.

As we know, from one end of the Arab-Islamic world to the other, architecture has brought the very notion of the door to its paroxysm. Whether it be arches with lambrequins or stalactites, polylobed or lanceolate arches, the adornments are of unrivalled refinement. Whether it be gateways to cities or neighborhoods, mosque or palace gates, the masterpieces are strictly speaking innumerable. Think only of the gates of the city of Fez or those of Cairo! Or the gates of the Alhambra Palace! Or the gate to the Aleppo Citadel, with its particularly complex plan! It is this extreme sophistication that is undermined by the images Moath Alofi offers of these square arches, comprising three metal facets. Their disconcerting simplicity somehow transcends the very notion of a door as it exists in the Arab-Islamic world and sublimates it by means of this impressive counter-example.

In fact, these holes only serve to open the building onto itself. But there is no denying that, above all, they open onto an elsewhere that has long been the subject of aspirations and dreams. Moath Alofi's gaze grants them access to another register, an almost tangible reality, offering a concrete expression of these dreams and aspirations within the geography of the Arabic peninsula, or a spiritual one within the precepts of religion. If they had long dreamt of their journey, if they then accomplished it within difficult or even painful conditions, as was most often the case, once they reached Bab al-Bunt, the travelers experimented a kind of climax, as though they had effectively reached the Gate of Gates!

When these openings were made is of little relevance, as it is not from a historical viewpoint that these "Iron Gates" are considered, but a symbolic one. To give us access to some very powerful perspectives, they simply need to be there, with their steel uprights, as Moath Alofi presents them to us.

ON THE VERGE OF ABSTRACTION

Beyond these elliptical hieratics, Moath Alofi has also focused on other walls. The photographer thus revived familiar practices from recent works, such as *Walls of Medina* (2016) or *Doors of Barlik* (2017). These past experiences enabled the photographer to hone his gaze; they taught him that walls can be deciphered like the pages of a palimpsest, layer after layer.

Moath Alofi is in search of the signs, traces, and marks that the walls of Bab al-Bunt bear. He knows it is easy to miss what he is looking for. The risk being, of course, not to see anything, when everything can depend on a shadow or an angle of view. Only a seasoned eye can detect what, at times, can be overly apparent or, on the contrary, seems to escape from view.

The photographer also knows that it matters little to present interpretations. Instead, it is better to provide clues, which will draw on the audience's imagination when they will see his works, leaving it up to them to make their own interpretations. This is how Moath Alofi wends his way between the walls of the building, coming and going, retracing his steps, tracing unforeseen itineraries from which he brings back bountiful images.

Some of these could, for instance, give rise to stimulating analogies. It all depends on the way in which they are considered, of course. There are nevertheless few efforts to be made to establish, based on several of these images, a correlation with the very ancient maps that the great Arab geographers of the classical centuries have left to us, which, in turn, allow the texts of famous travelers from these same eras to be evoked, such as Ibn Battuta, Ibn Fadlan, Ibn Jubayr... These comparisons are made by those who, among the audience of these images, let themselves be won over by their playful dimension. It is not even clear whether these comparisons were intended by the author of these photographs. The main thing is that he was able to make them possible.

Every image is the consequence of a moment of pause, when the photographer was able to be interpellated by a scratch on the wall, the fall of a plaster plate, a few stains of paint, graffiti, or a sunbeam on the floor... It is in this way – through these signs, marks, and traces that may seem minuscule – that, on the verge of abstraction, a kind of geography or cosmography is set up, in the maze of which Moath Alofi invites us to follow him.

In this way, the photographer draws new maps. He holds out the pages of a new book to us, with each page seeming capable of explaining a part of the mystery contained in these walls. And when we have read this book and considered these images, the feeling would dawn in us of having penetrated the spirit of the place, as we now held the keys granting us access to its history.

PARAPHERNALIA

In his description of the place, the photographer also chose to embark on another path. As we have already noted, Moath Alofi initially respected the emptiness that stood out for him on his wanderings within the building.

However, this vacancy hardly impressed him, no doubt thanks to the complicity he has developed with desert landscapes in several of his works – and notably *People of Pangaea* (2018) and *Mihlaiel* (2018). Moath Alofi knows that this vacancy is a lure.

That is because this emptiness is populated by many remainders, scattered and disparate elements that escaped the labor of the movers. These forgotten objects, stubbornly resisting removal, were to allow Moath Alofi to give his humor and virtuosity free rein; they too, in their own way, constitute signs, traces, and marks that the photographer would latch onto.

Most of these objects were left on the floor, some have remained attached to the walls. Chance alone has governed their fate. No staging was undertaken. No adjustment. No addition. Such are the implicit rules of the game that the photographer maintained. It gives the project its pertinence. Moath Alofi has modified nothing, photographing the spaces of al-Bunt as he found them. It was no doubt necessary to stick to appearances in order to better surpass them later.

The list of these objects consists of a long inventory, not devoid of a poetic element. They are sometimes presented in groups. For instance, a set of frames. Another of amulets. Or of feathers from an unidentified

Carsten Niebuhr
Map of the city of Jeddah, 1776
From *Voyage en Arabie et en d'autres pays circonvoisins* [Travel to Arabia and other neighboring countries],
vol. 1, tab. LV, translated from German by F.L. Mourier and published by S.J. Baalde, Amsterdam, 1776
Collection of the Saudi Ministry of Culture, PT 2019.28a

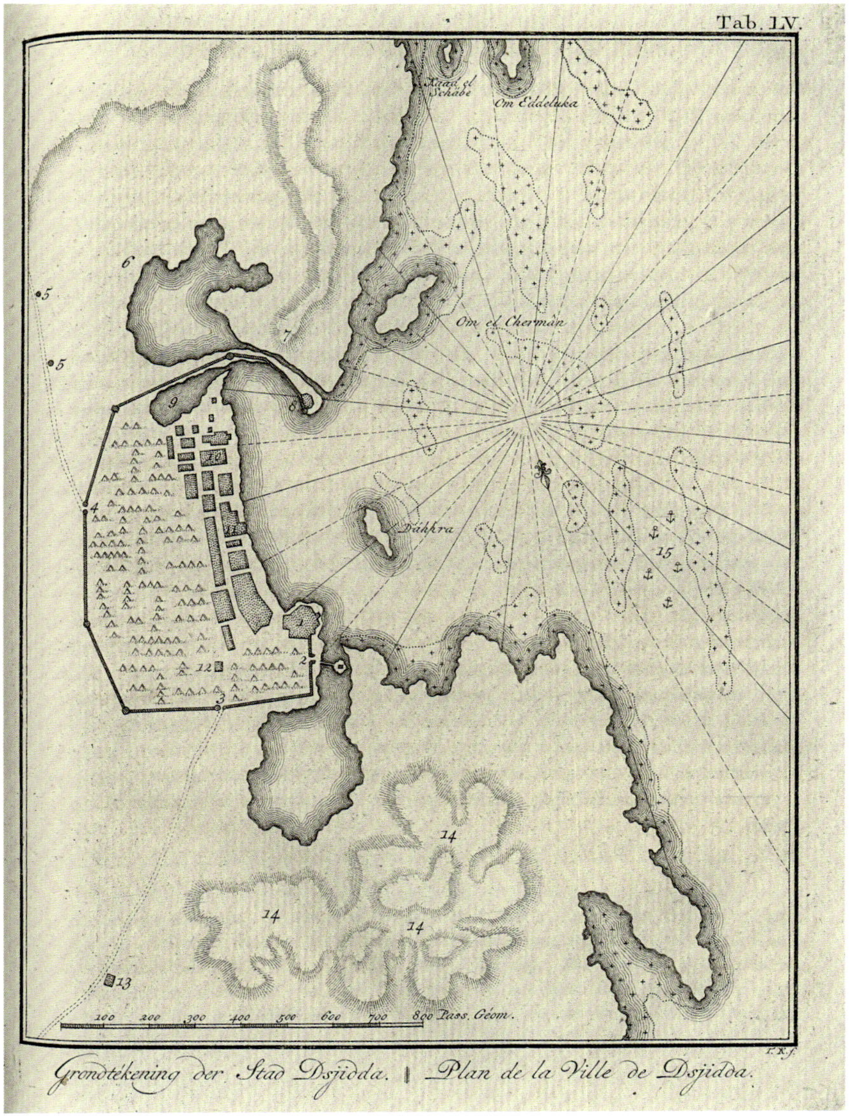

bird – perhaps a pigeon – which could well form the reliefs of ancient feasts. They also come in pairs. Two fans, for instance... Two sticks of incense. Or in isolation. As is the case of a rosary. Sunglasses. An obsolete form from the governorate of the city of Jeddah... Or sometimes they form curious couples. A rubber ball and a plastic hanger find themselves paired... Naturally, they are reminiscent of the famous phrase by French poet Isidore Ducasse, Count of Lautréamont, in his *Songs of Maldoror*, evoking "the fortuitous encounter of a sewing machine and an umbrella on a dissecting table," of which the surrealists were so fond.

A chair. A simple plastic chair. Perhaps one of the most notable images by Moath Alofi. The chair is empty. As is the one in one of the most illustrious canvases of pictorial modernity: Van Gogh's *Bedroom in Arles* (1888). A simple chair features there as well, whose seat is made of straw. Empty. Picasso, Matisse – to name but a few – would later paint the same subject. An ordinary straw chair. With a century between them, it is the exact equivalent of this plastic chair, an example of which Moath Alofi is careful to show us. Known as a Monobloc, due to the fact that plastic is injected into it – in this case, polypropylene – as a single mold, its manufacture requires no assembly. It has been mass-produced, all over the planet, since the early 1970s, to the point of becoming emblematic of our age. Everyone, or nearly everyone, owns at least one, in their garden, workshop, or even their apartment. Consequently, we understand that it often crops up in the artworks of some of the greatest contemporary artists. This is how it is represented – empty – in the paintings of the American Alex Katz (*Beach Scenes and Landscapes*, 2002), or the Romanian Adrian Ghenie (*The Picnic*, 2015), to cite just these two. The image that Moath Alofi presents to us of this chair, forgotten between the walls of al-Bunt, is remarkable on all counts, and in particular from a chromatic point of view. It is part of a broader approach, in which it naturally finds its place.

Then there are also big, massive bundles that could not go unnoticed by the photographer! Abandoned in a corner of al-Bunt. Enormous... Yet, this imposing character and this weight are immediately belied, contradicted, by another aspect, namely the obviously childlike appearance of printed designs featured on the cotton fabric covering these improbable balloons, infusing them with a certain lightness. Properly naming them is not easy: balls, bundles, balloons, packets, kits. It is also impossible to say what they contain, nothing provides any indication. But they are there. And, not without irony, Moath Alofi presents them to our gaze. Perhaps their goal is to express something about the very long commercial past of the city of Jeddah and its port, whose development dates back to the mid-tenth century and the decline of the Abbasids of Baghdad. For a thousand years after that, the prosperity of Jeddah has virtually never been denied, as the many testimonies of travelers attest, admirative of the opulence of its souks.

The reception, accommodation, supply, and conveyance of the pilgrims certainly contributed to Jeddah's wealth. However, the huge fortune of the city, for all those centuries, was due above all to the scope of its trade. Coffee bundles, from Yemen. Tea bundles, from India. Grain bundles, from Egypt. All of these goods, and many others, were unloaded in the port of Jeddah, then reloaded, departing for other destinations. For all of these goods, customs duties were to be paid in a building located where Bab al-Bunt is today. The images of these strange bundles therefore suggest something about this other source of wealth that was continually Jeddah's, making the city the principal port in the region and even, at certain periods, of the whole Middle East.

*

The photographs of Bab al-Bunt that Moath Alofi presents fall within the direct line of research that he has carried out from his early works up until the most recent. His research, focusing on Arabia – from prehistoric times to the contemporary period – takes the human dimension into account as much as the religious, or even, we might say, the mythological dimensions, since the photographer makes the choice of slipping into the position of a chronicler – in the traditional sense of the term – of the history of Arabia from its origins.

Nonetheless, in his approach to the subjects that concern him, Moath Alofi manages to reconcile two attitudes that at first may appear antagonistic: on the one hand, knowing how to keep his subjects at a distance; and on the other, demonstrating an engagement with them that is very personal.

This is how, depending on the case, he can draw on different registers, such as those of empathy and humor, without relinquishing the formal character that underpins his approach. This way of proceeding is precisely the one he uses on his visit to al-Bunt, when he broaches a certain number of themes, the eclecticism of which is not of the sort to detract from the coherence emanating from a set of photographs that constitute a new episode of this chronicle in the history of Arabia that Moath Alofi simultaneously launched with his artistic career and that is deeply entwined with his oeuvre.

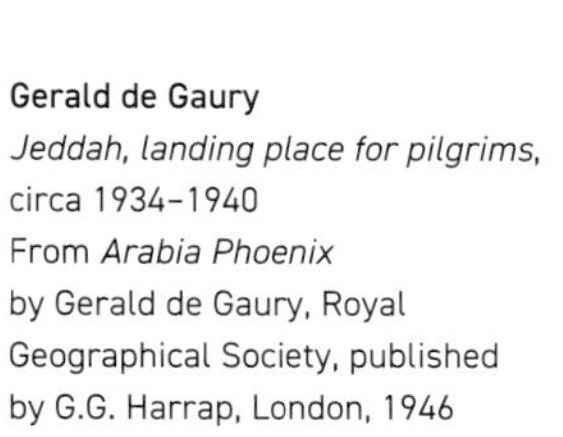

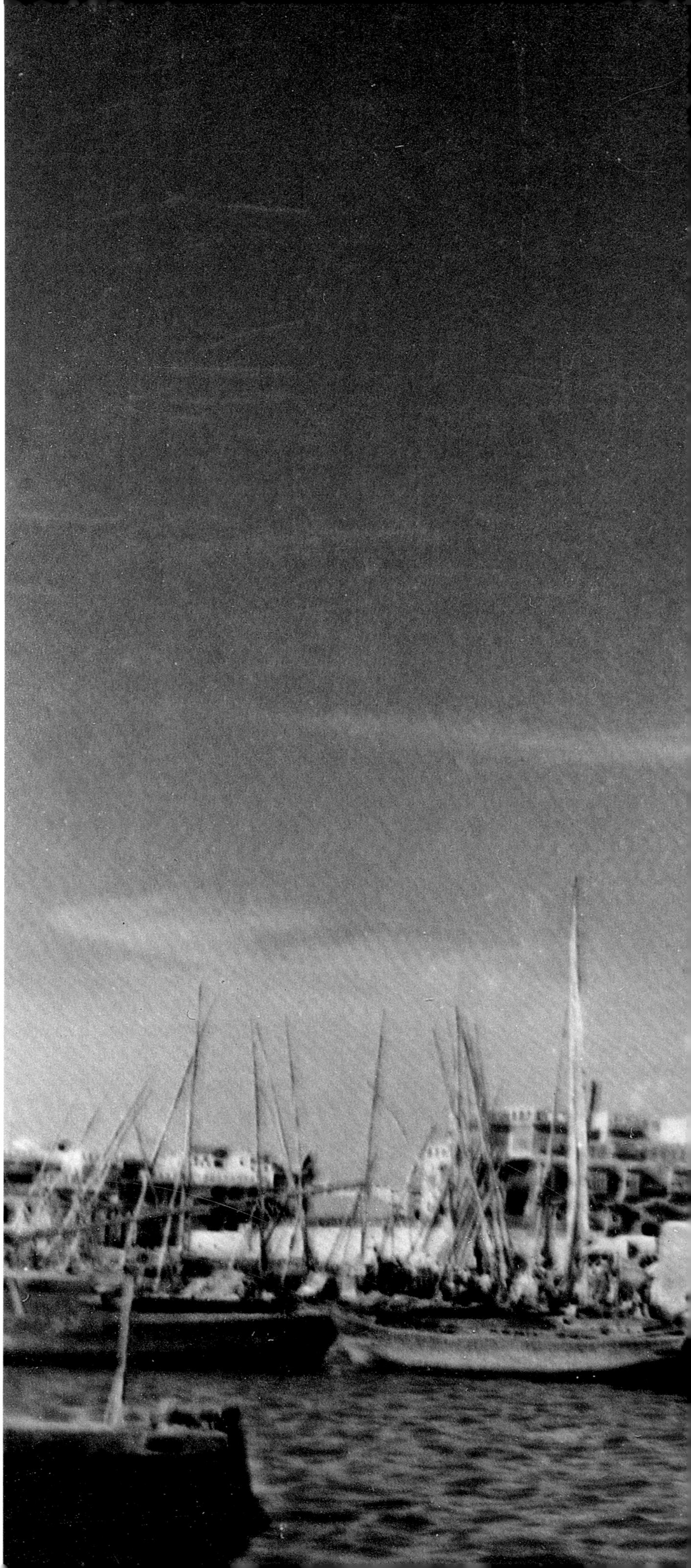

Gerald de Gaury
Jeddah, landing place for pilgrims,
circa 1934–1940
From *Arabia Phoenix*
by Gerald de Gaury, Royal
Geographical Society, published
by G.G. Harrap, London, 1946

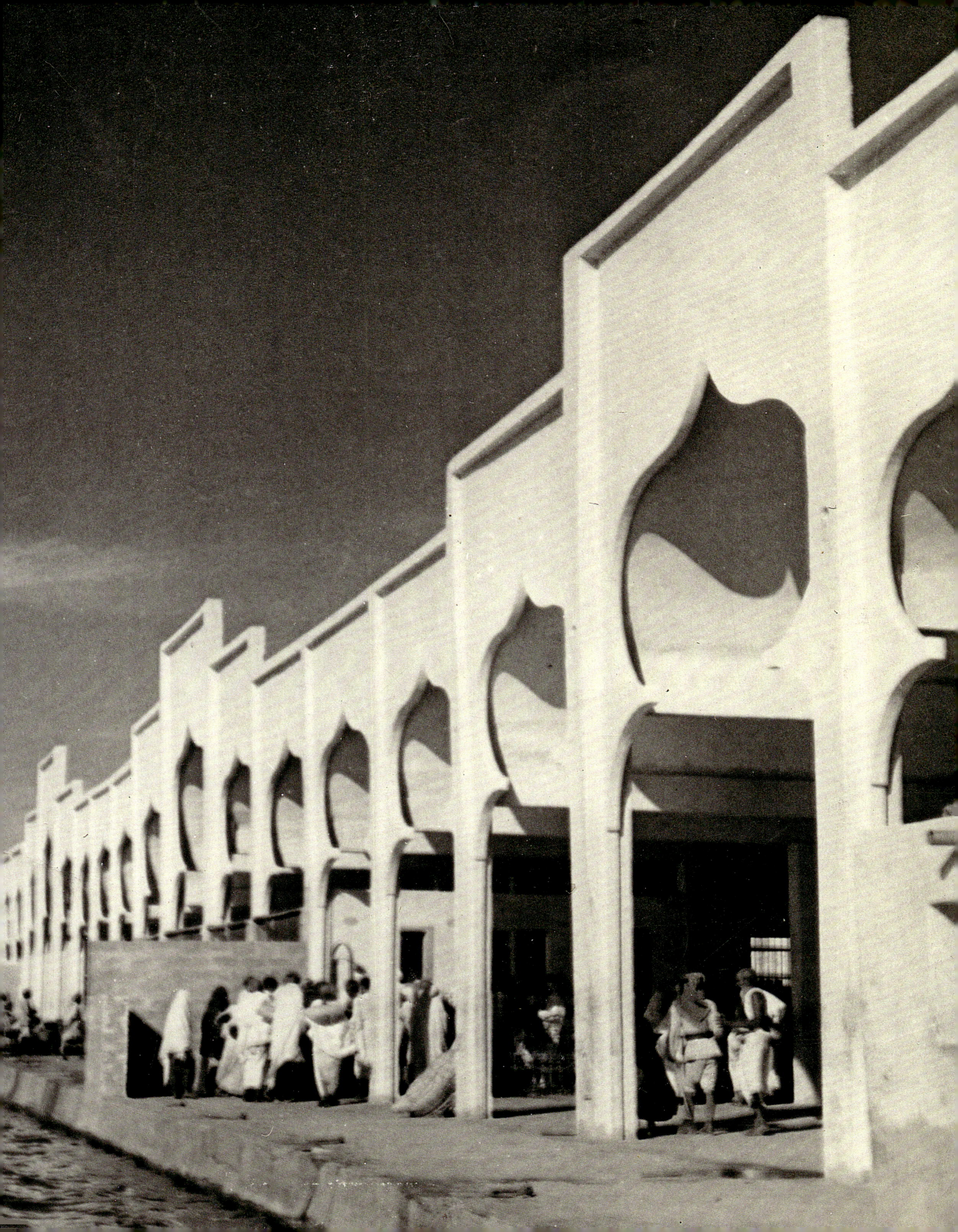

I.

The Spaces of al-Bunt

*A serenity emanates from these images
that may first appear cold, almost glacial,
but an intense vibration wells up
as we consider them.*

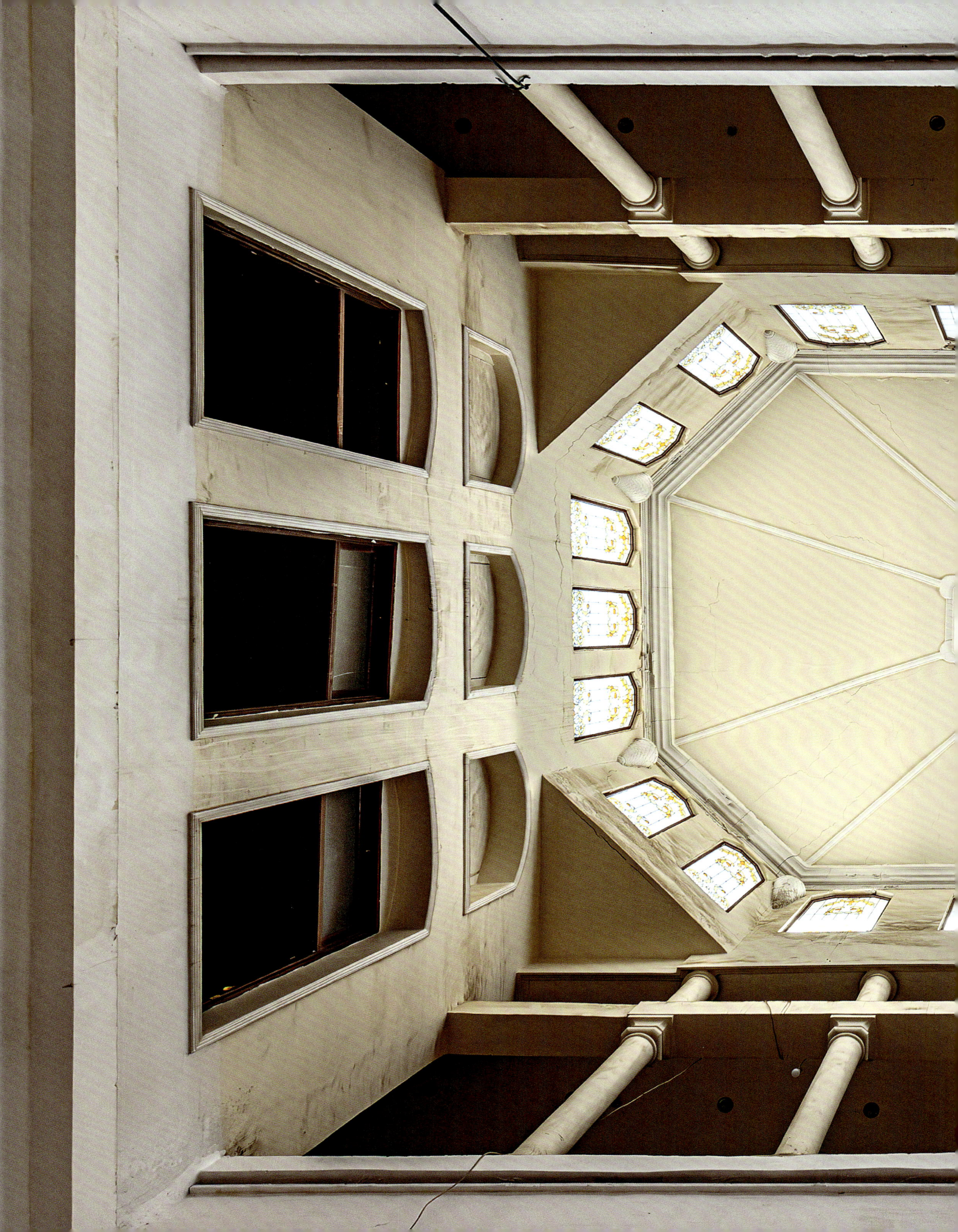

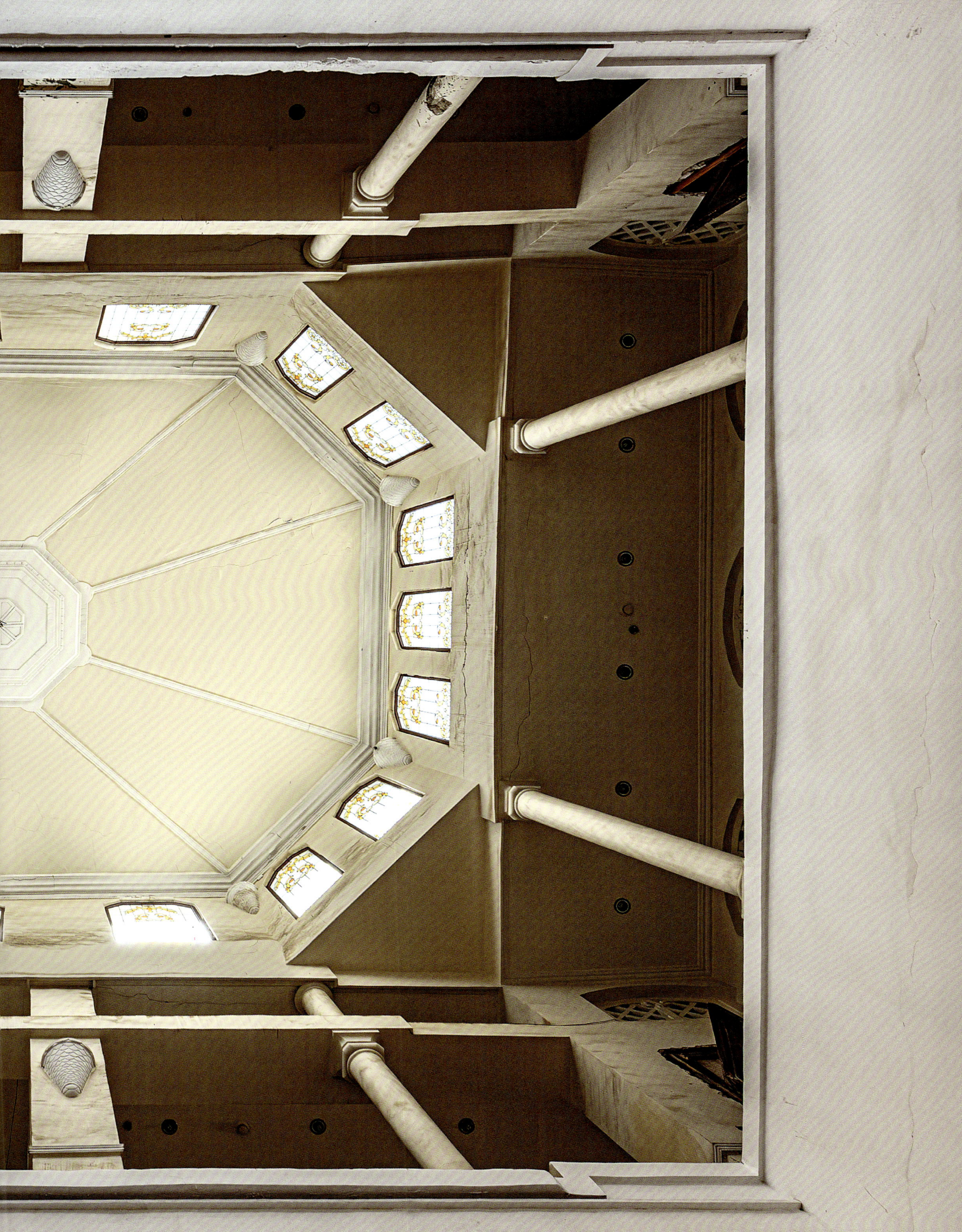

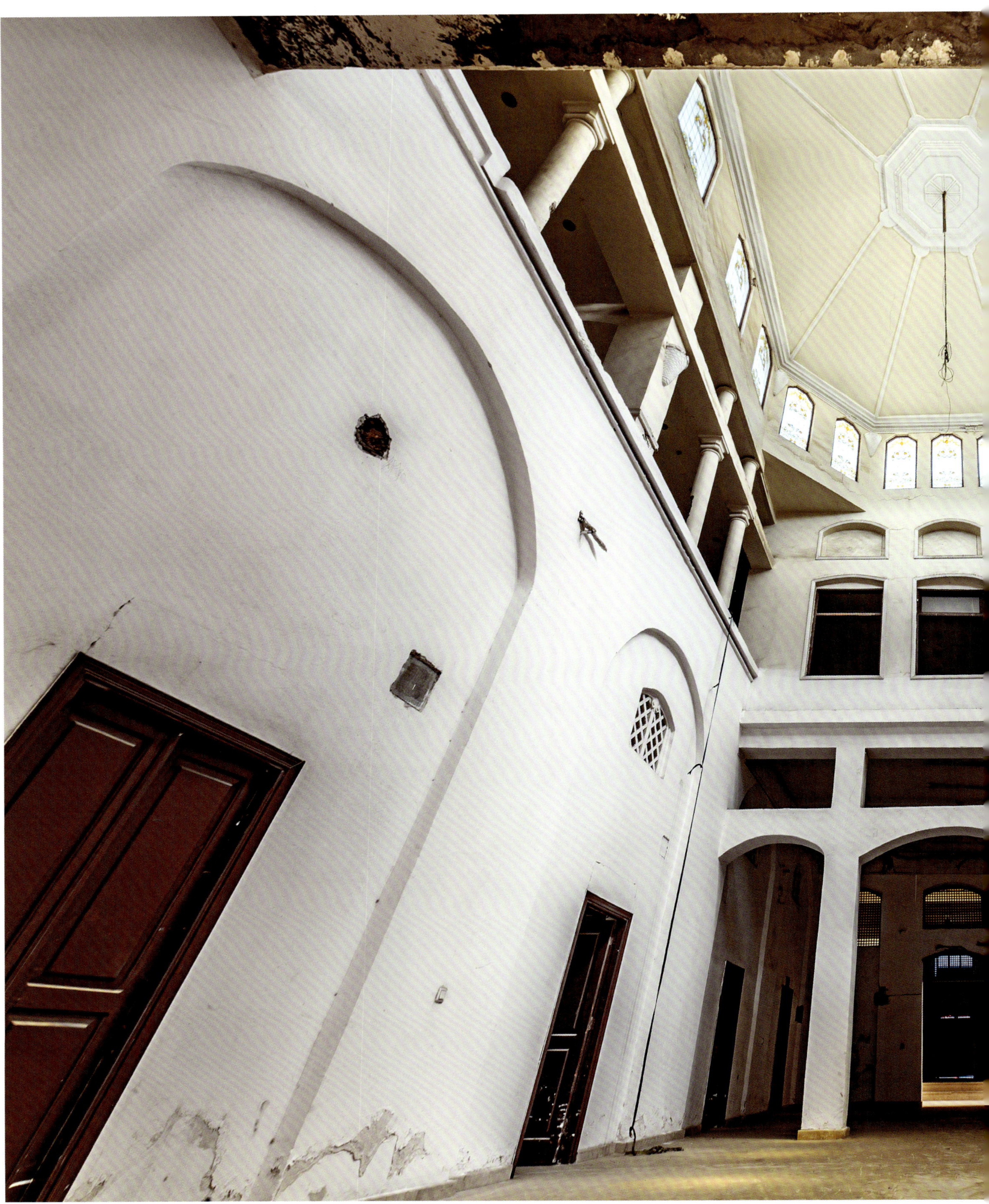

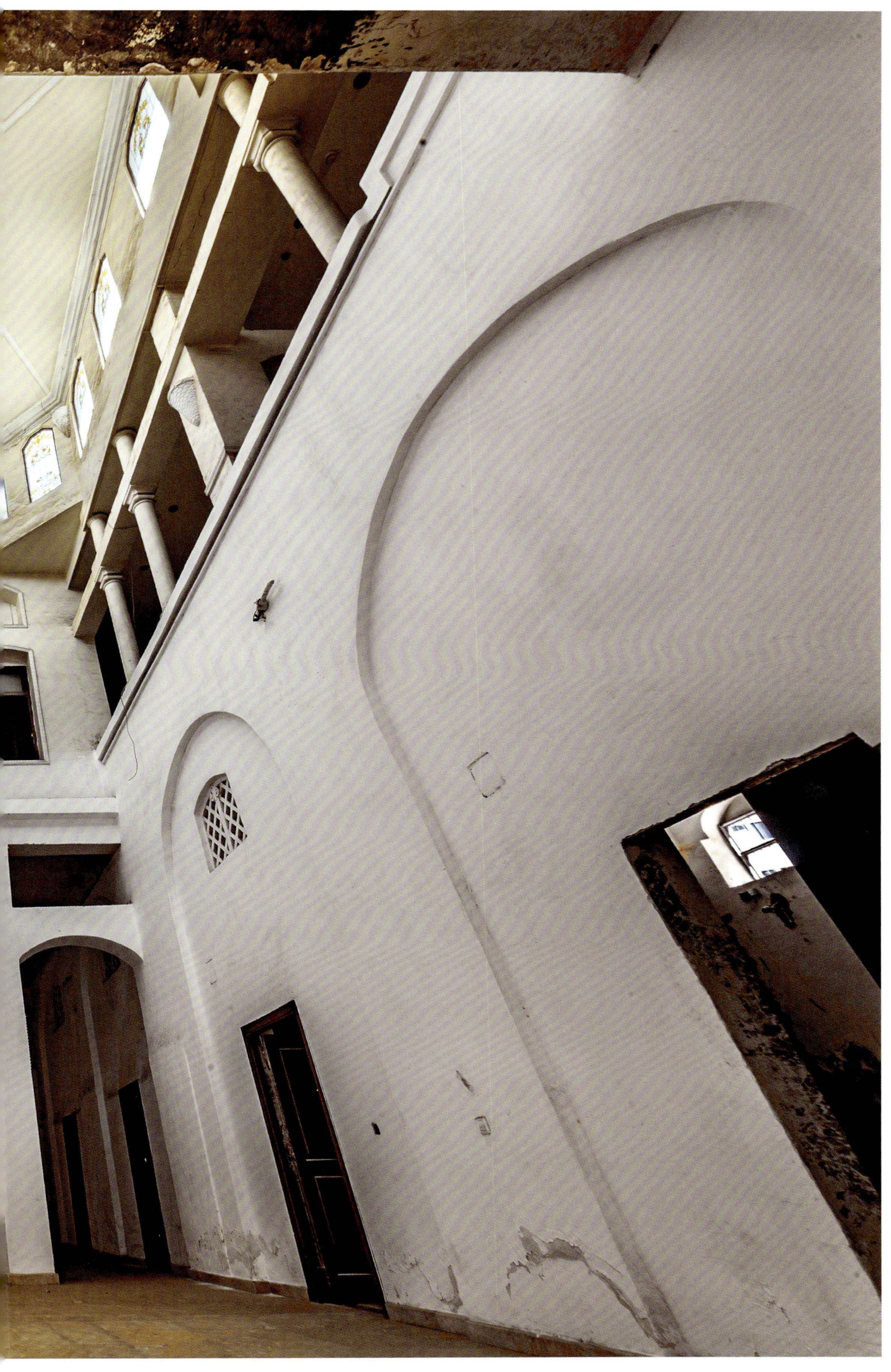

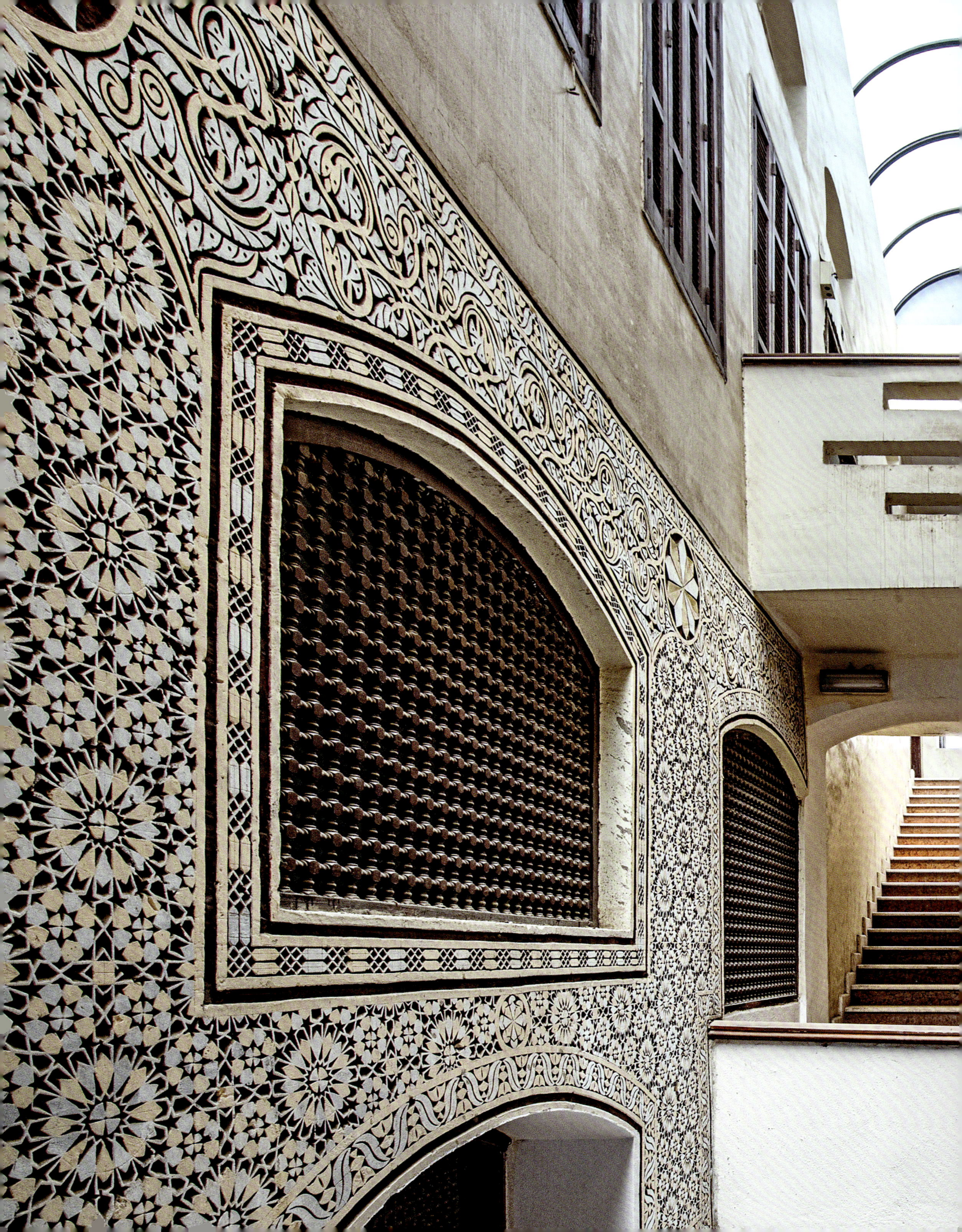

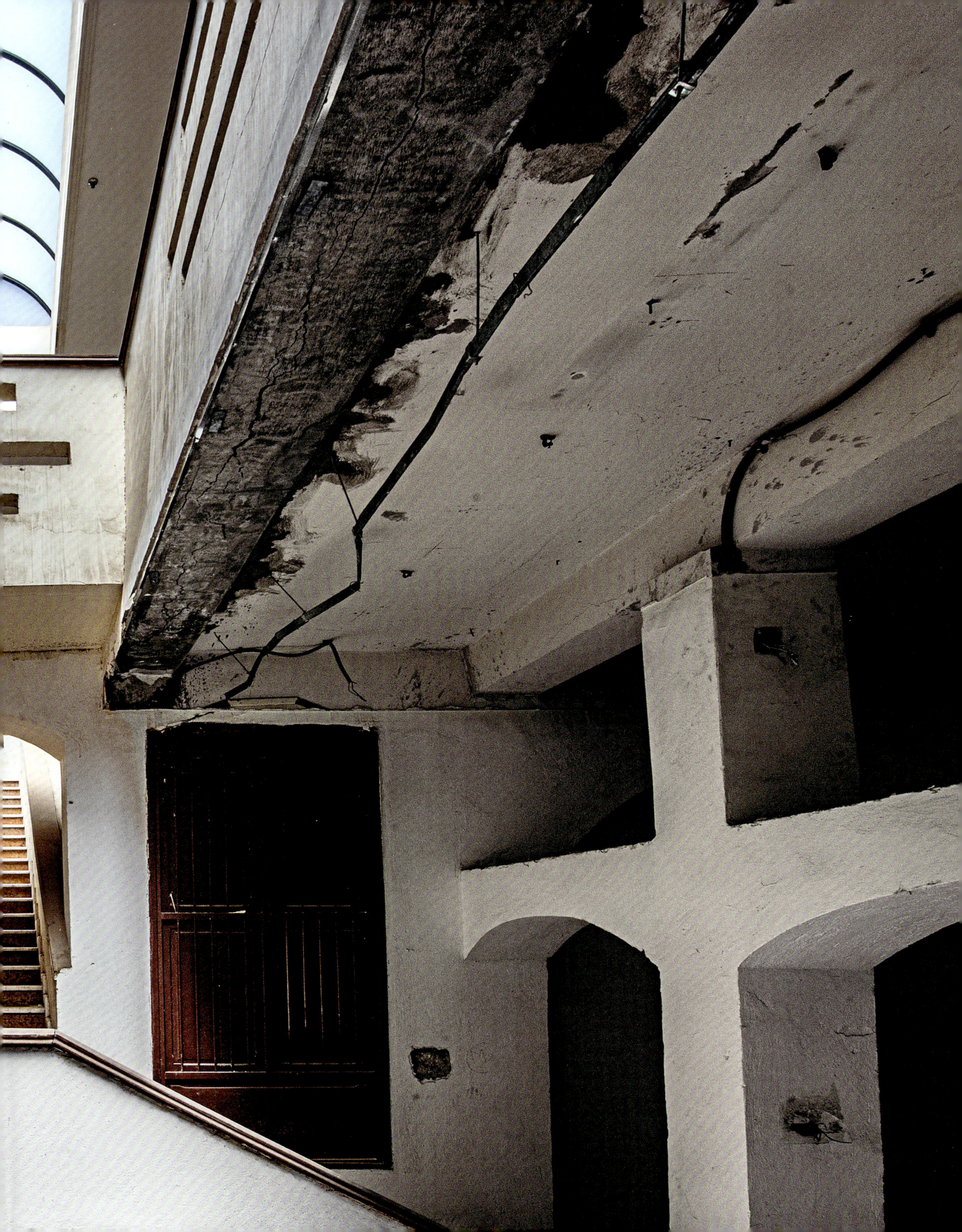

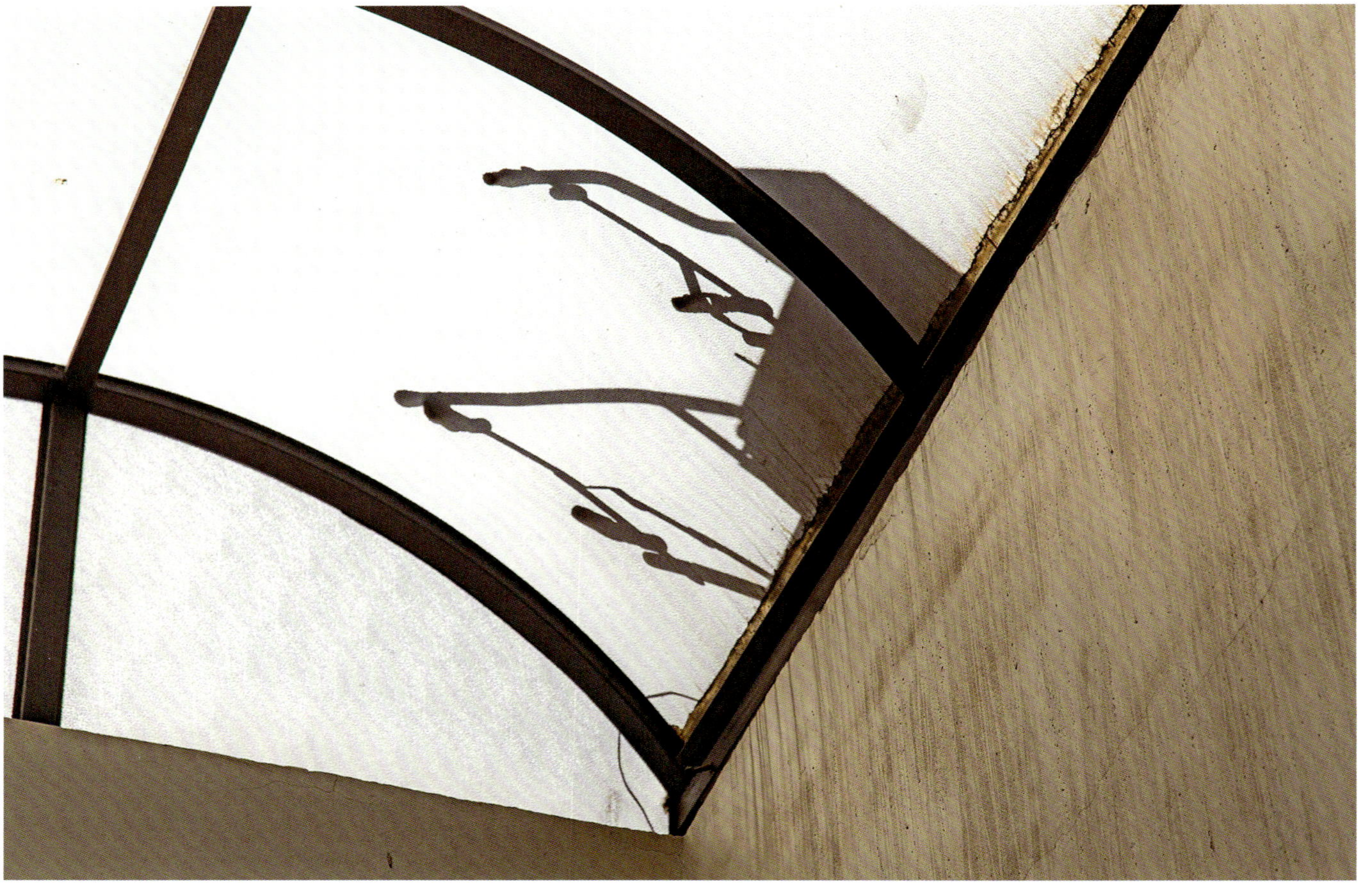

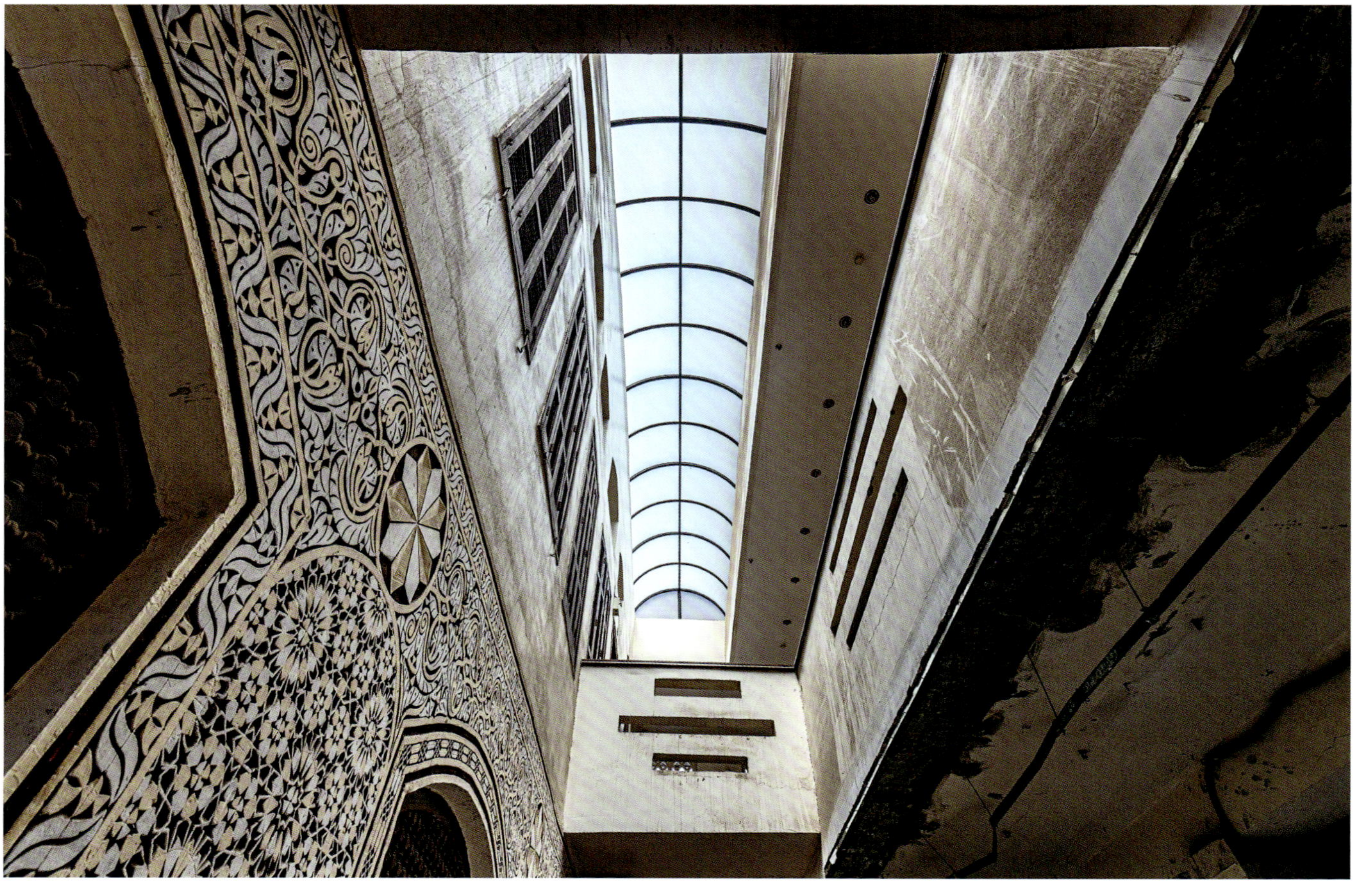

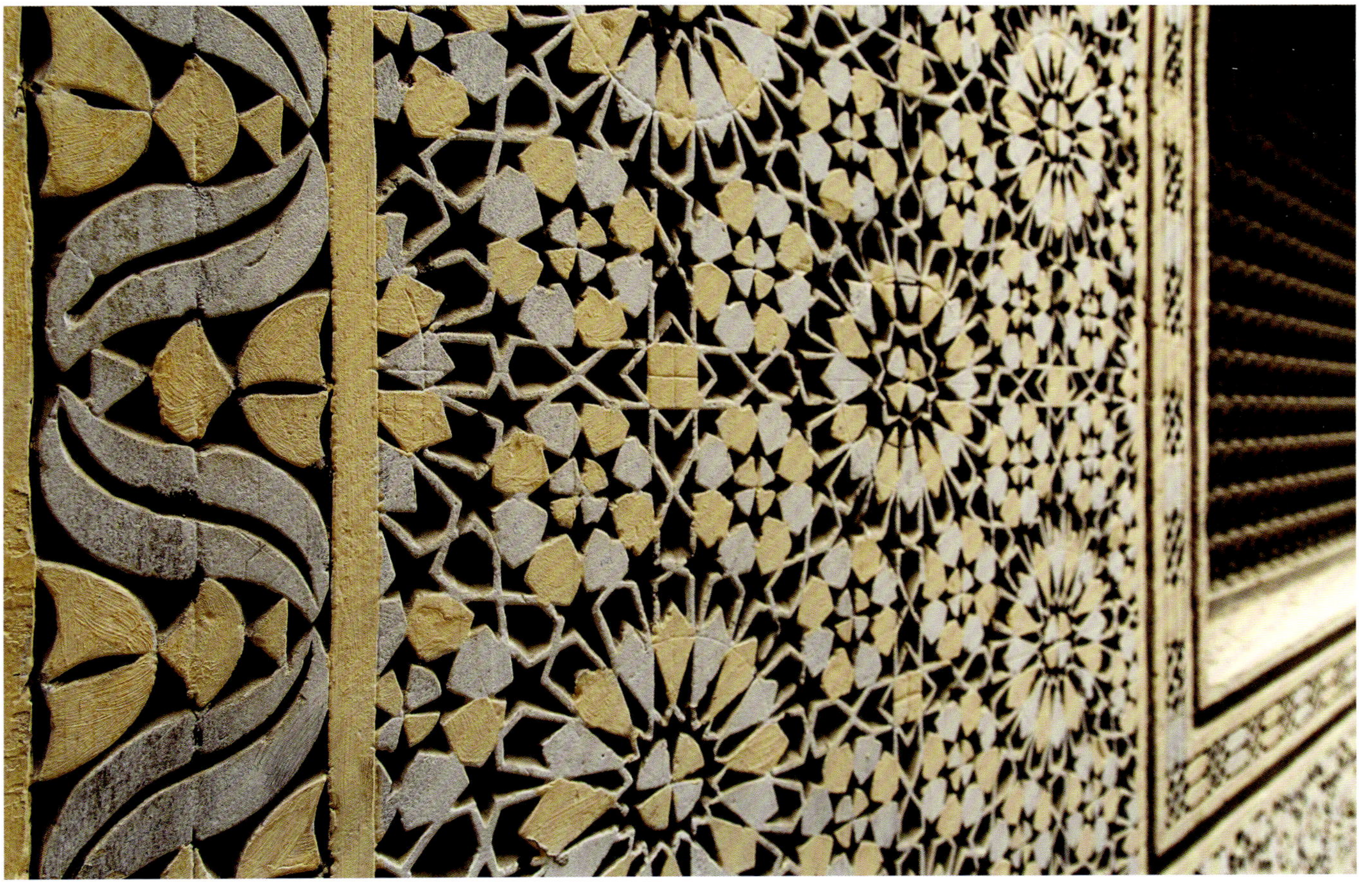

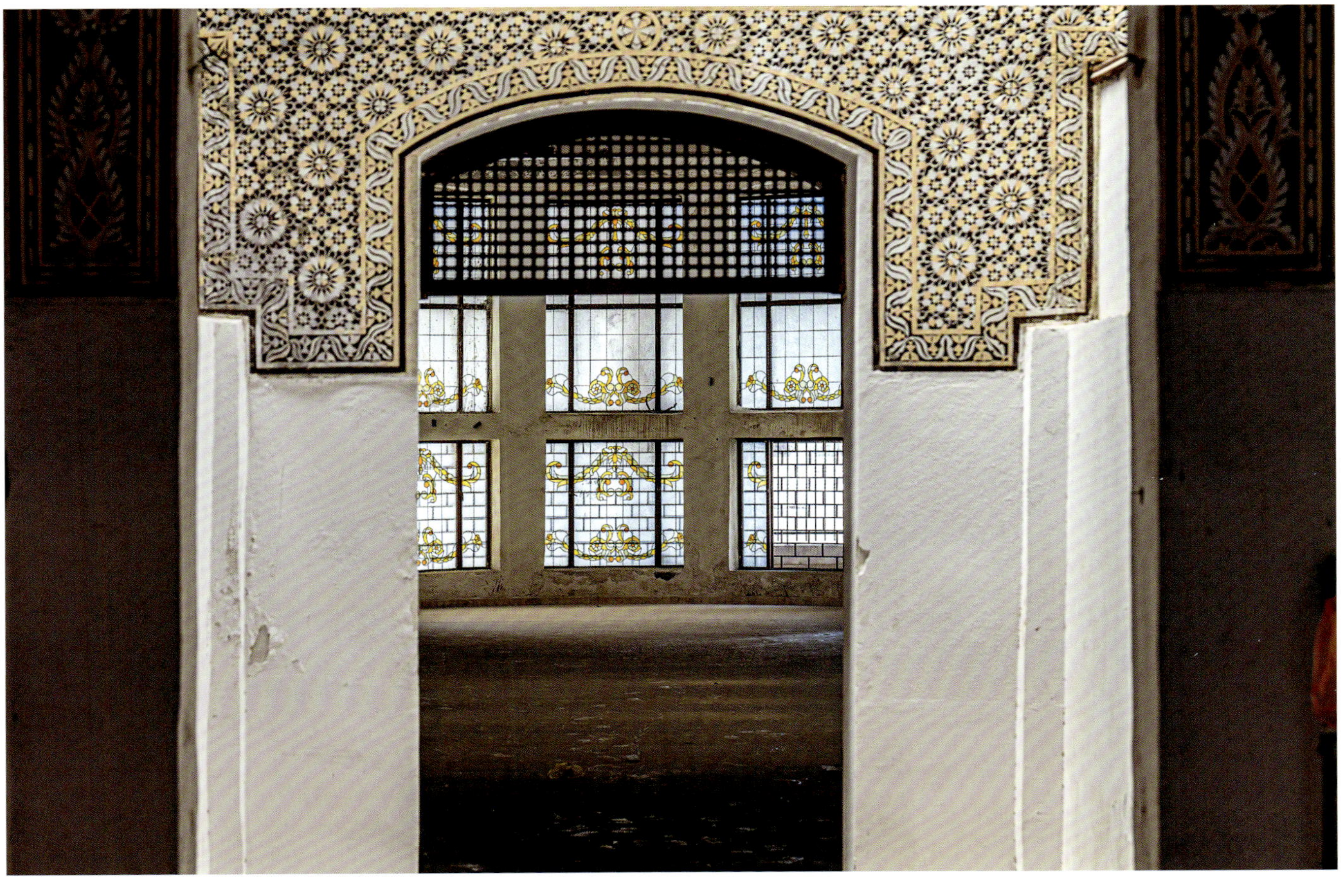

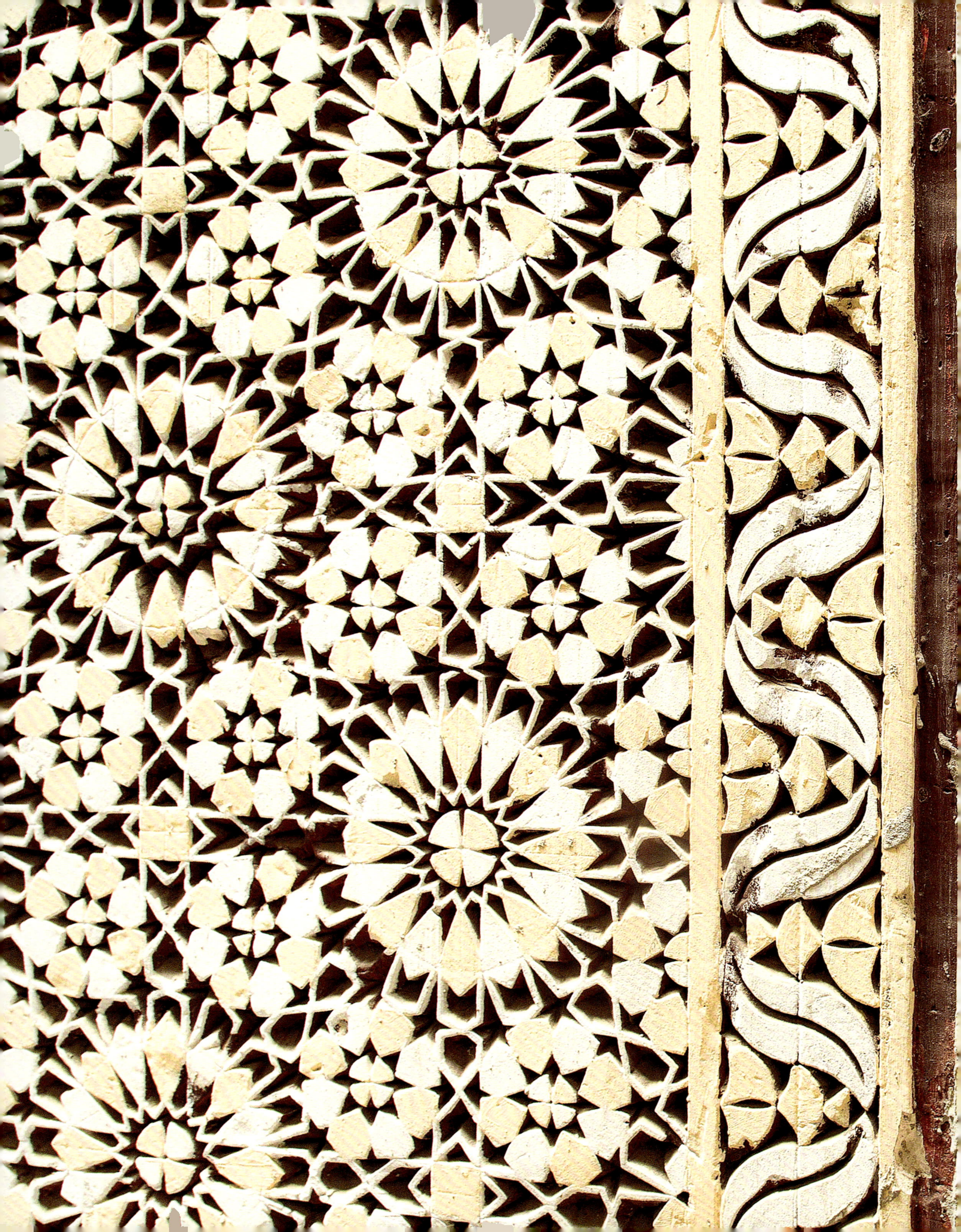

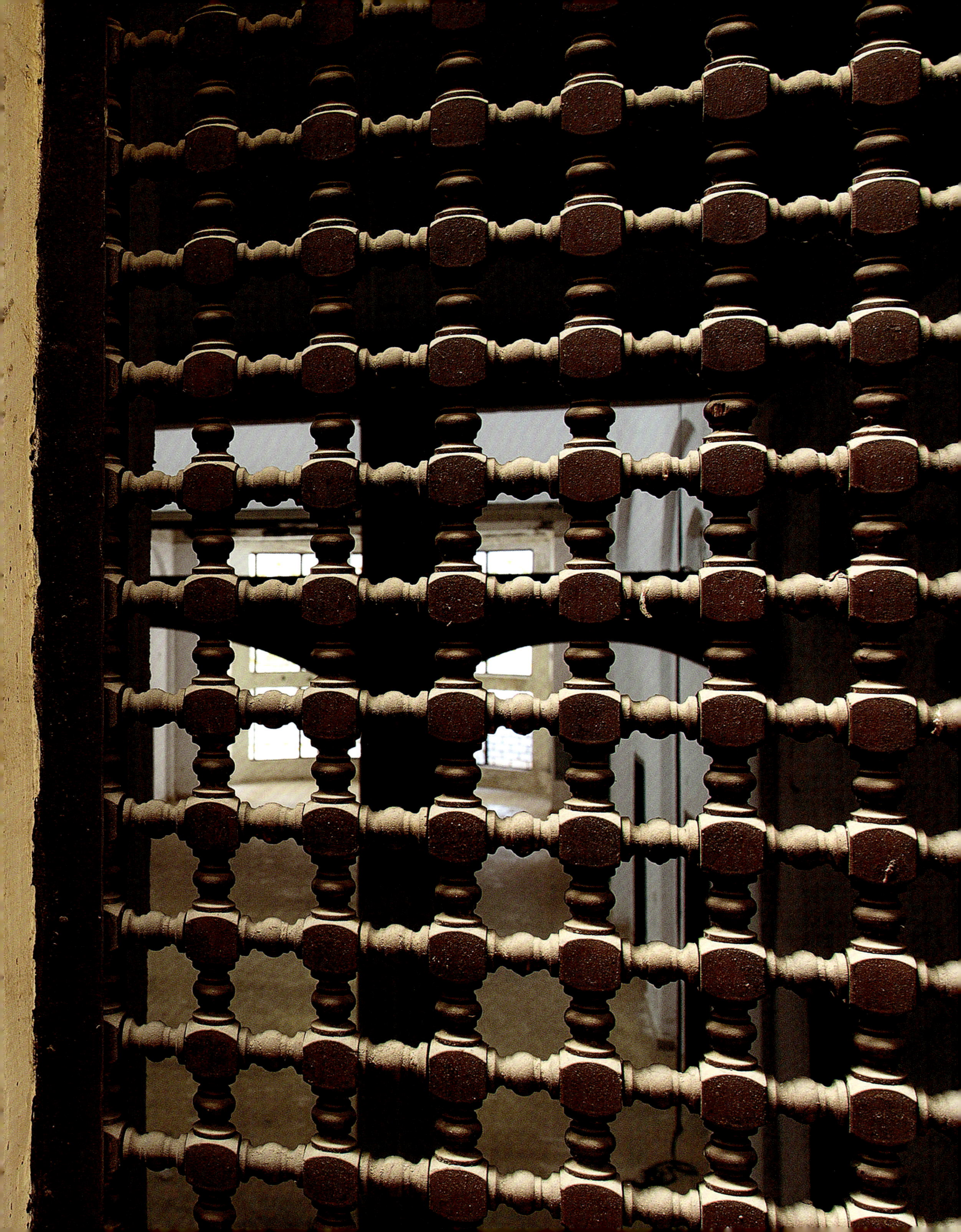

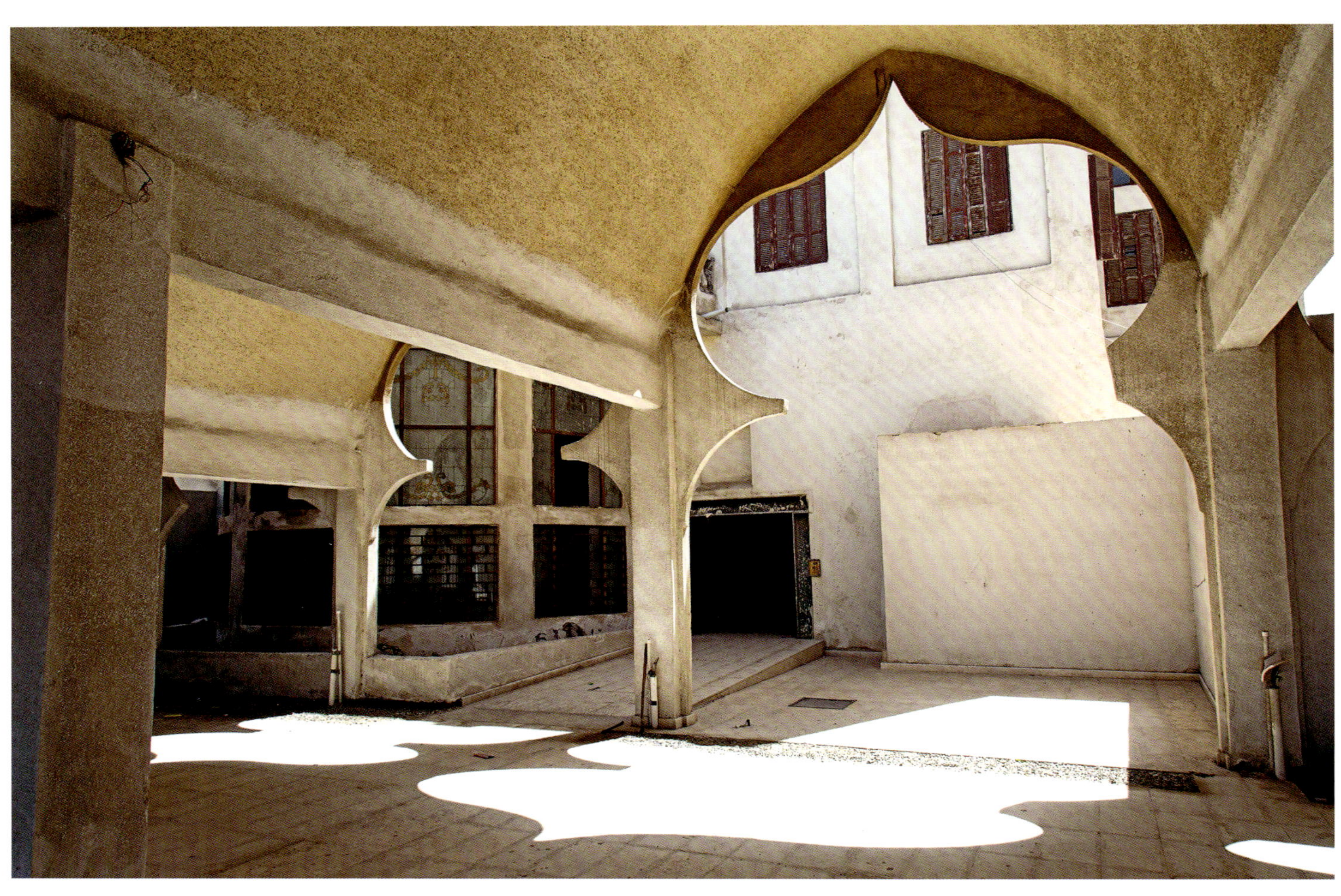

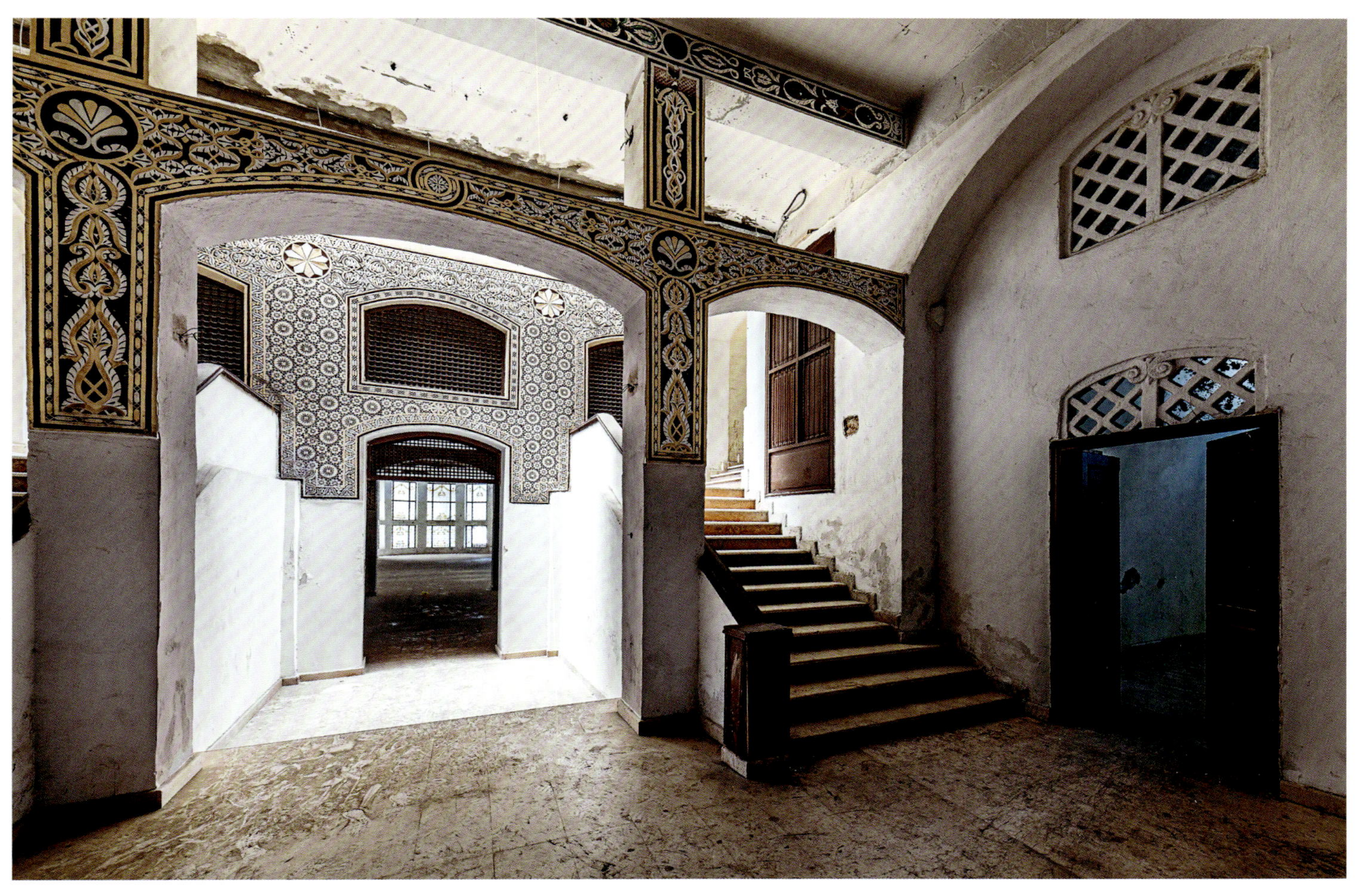

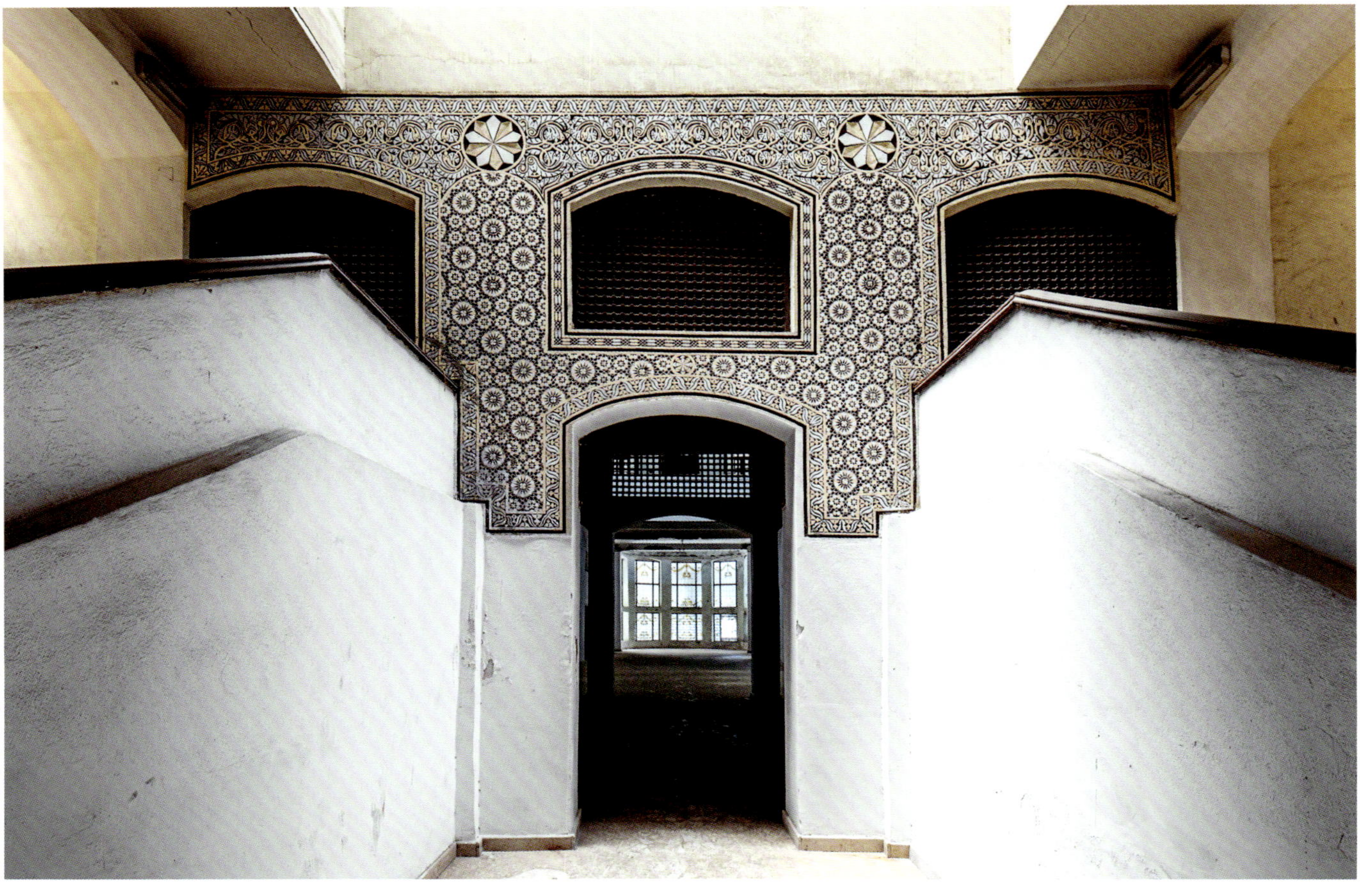

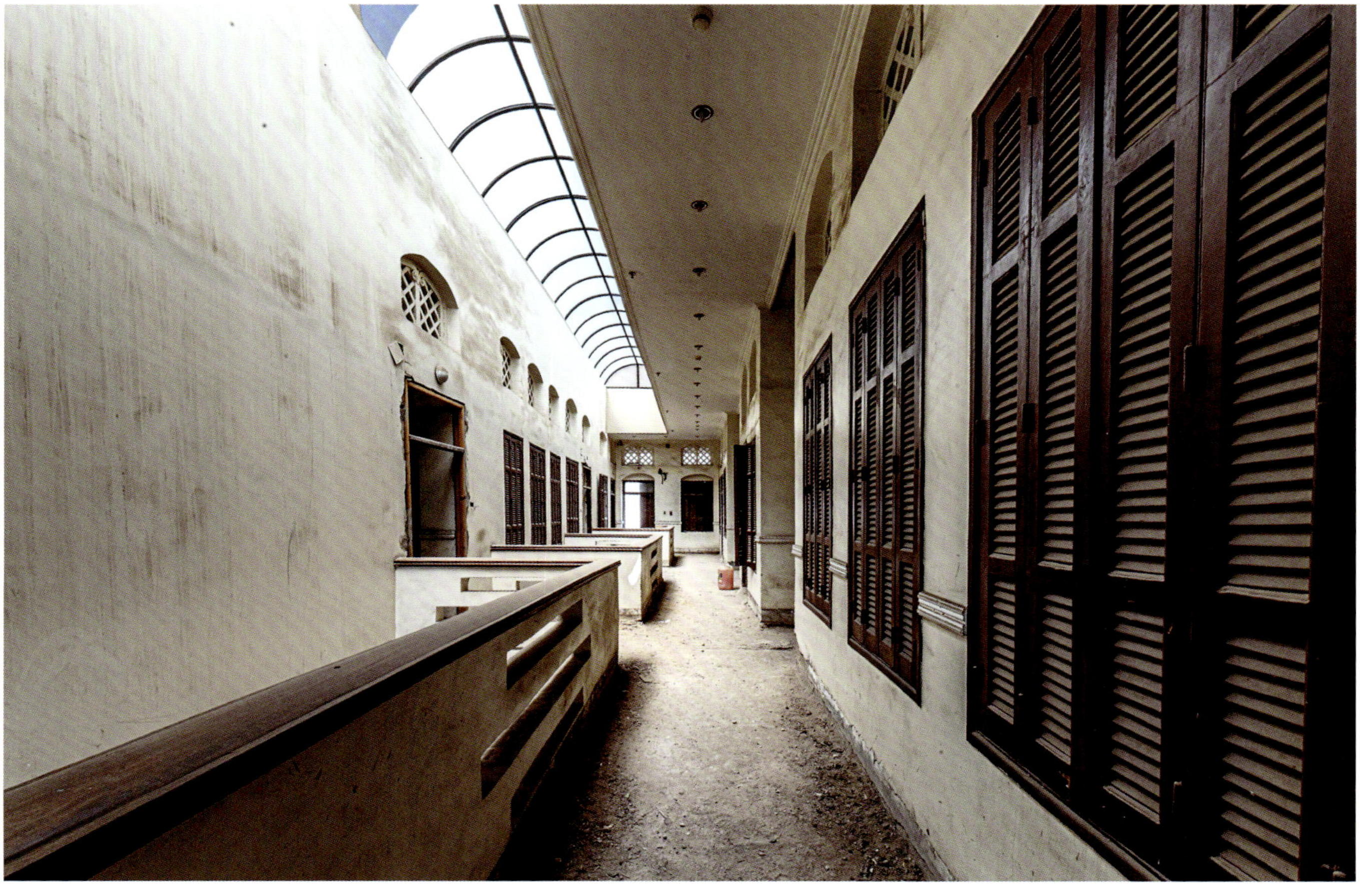

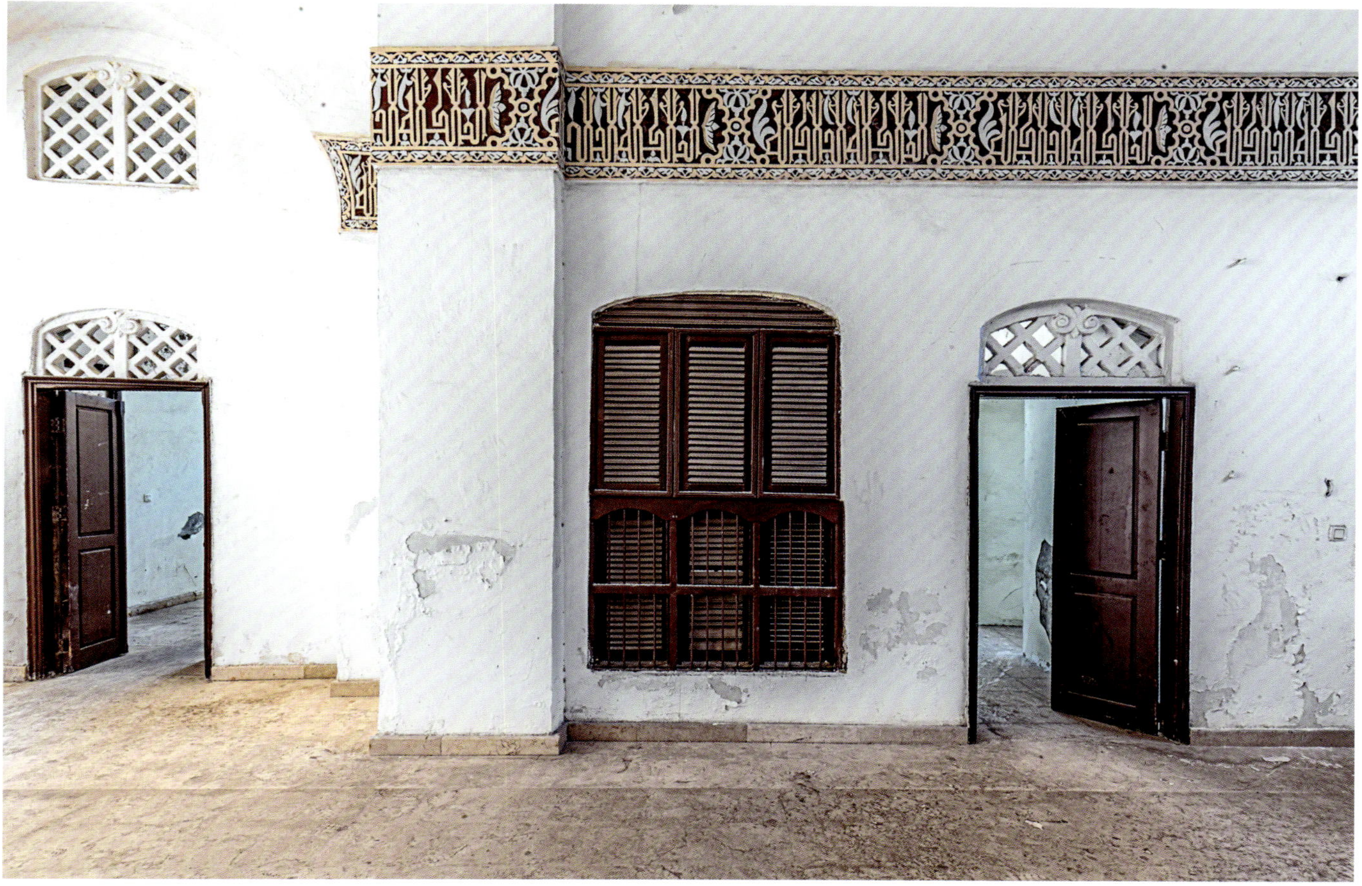

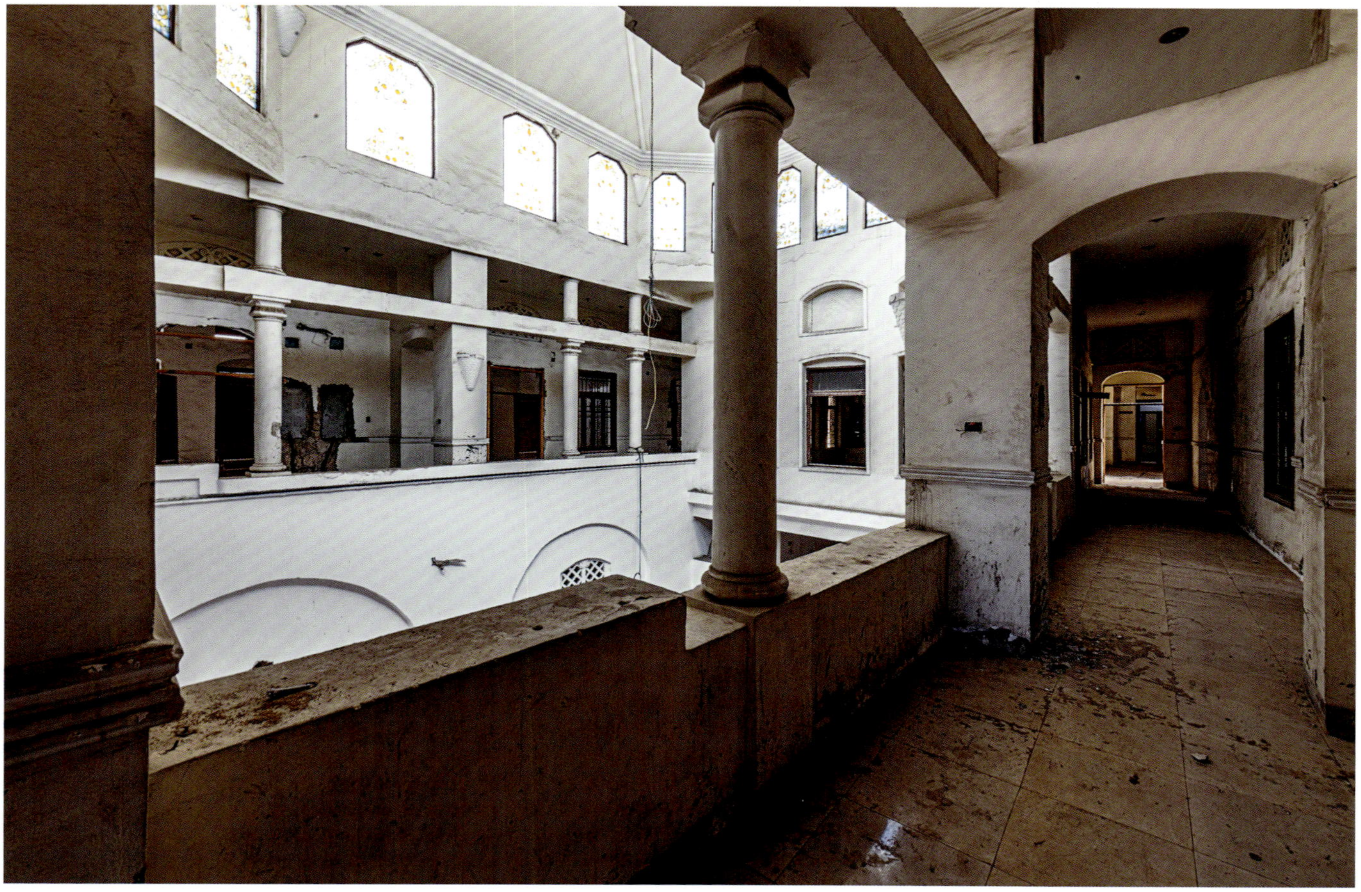

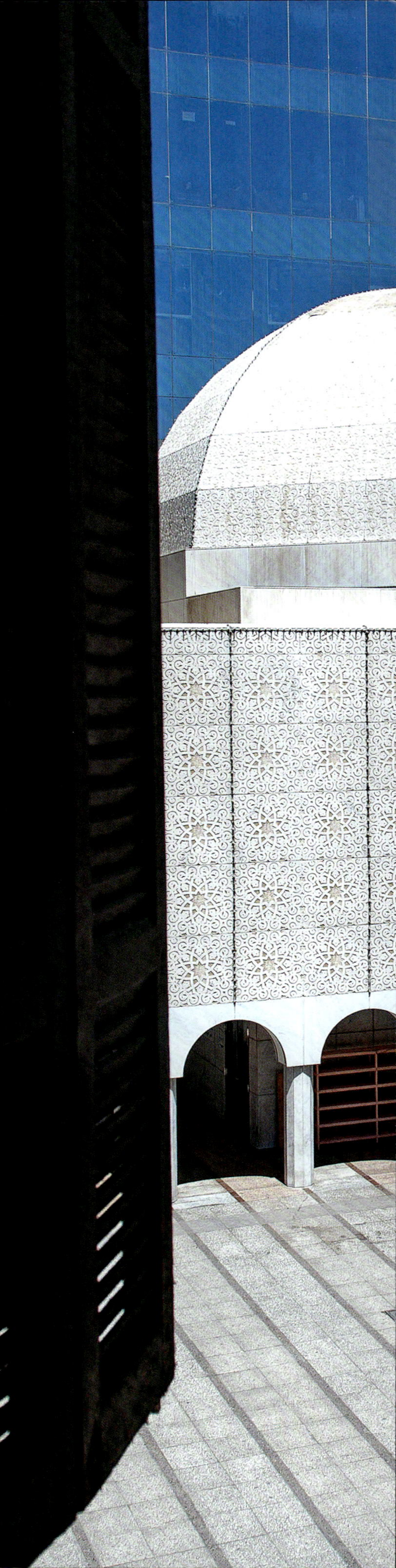

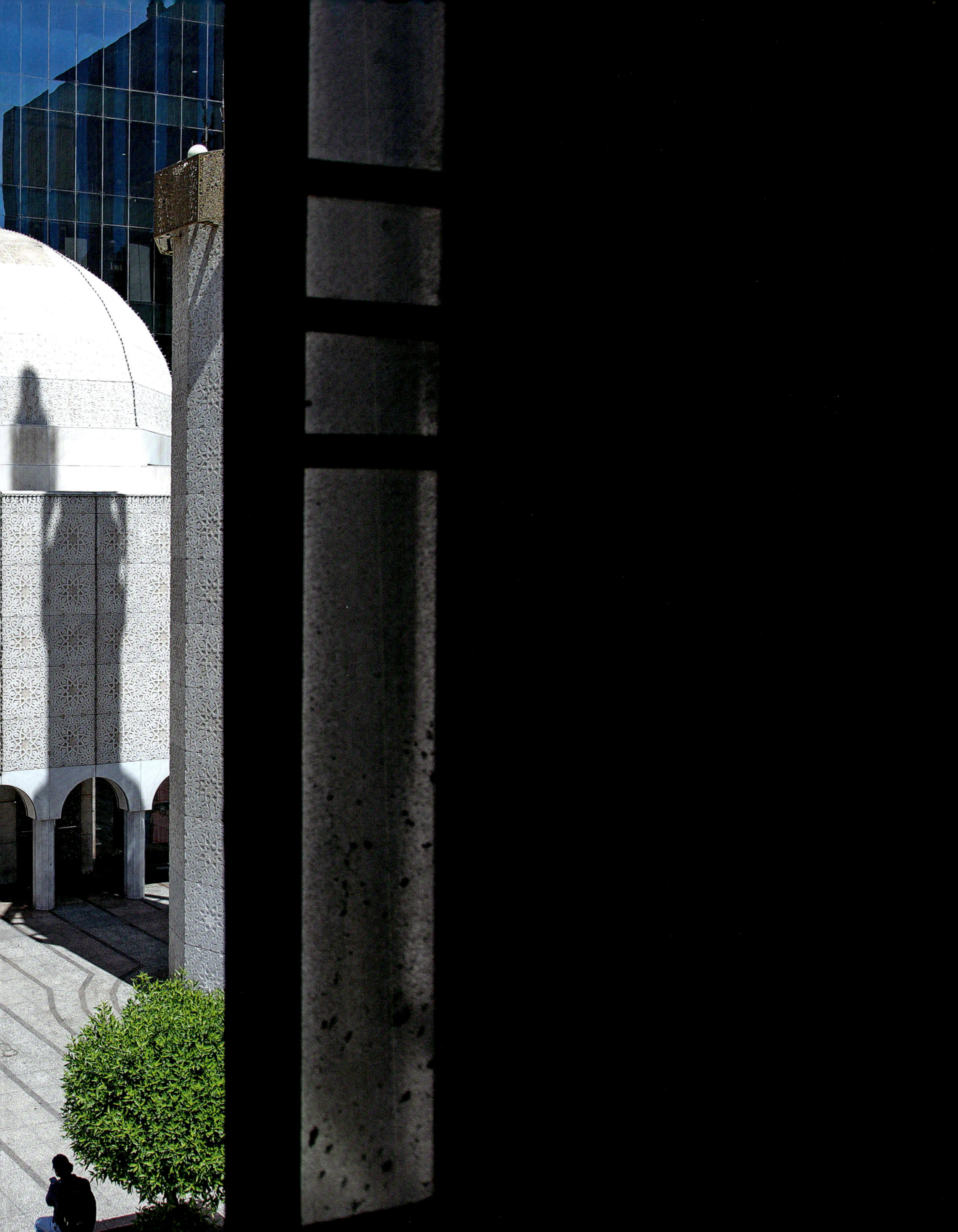

II.

The Iron Gates

If these are doors, they are of the utterly allegorical variety. Gateway to Jeddah. Gateway to Hejaz. Gateway to Arabia. Gateway to Pilgrimage. This is precisely what these photographs might suggest.

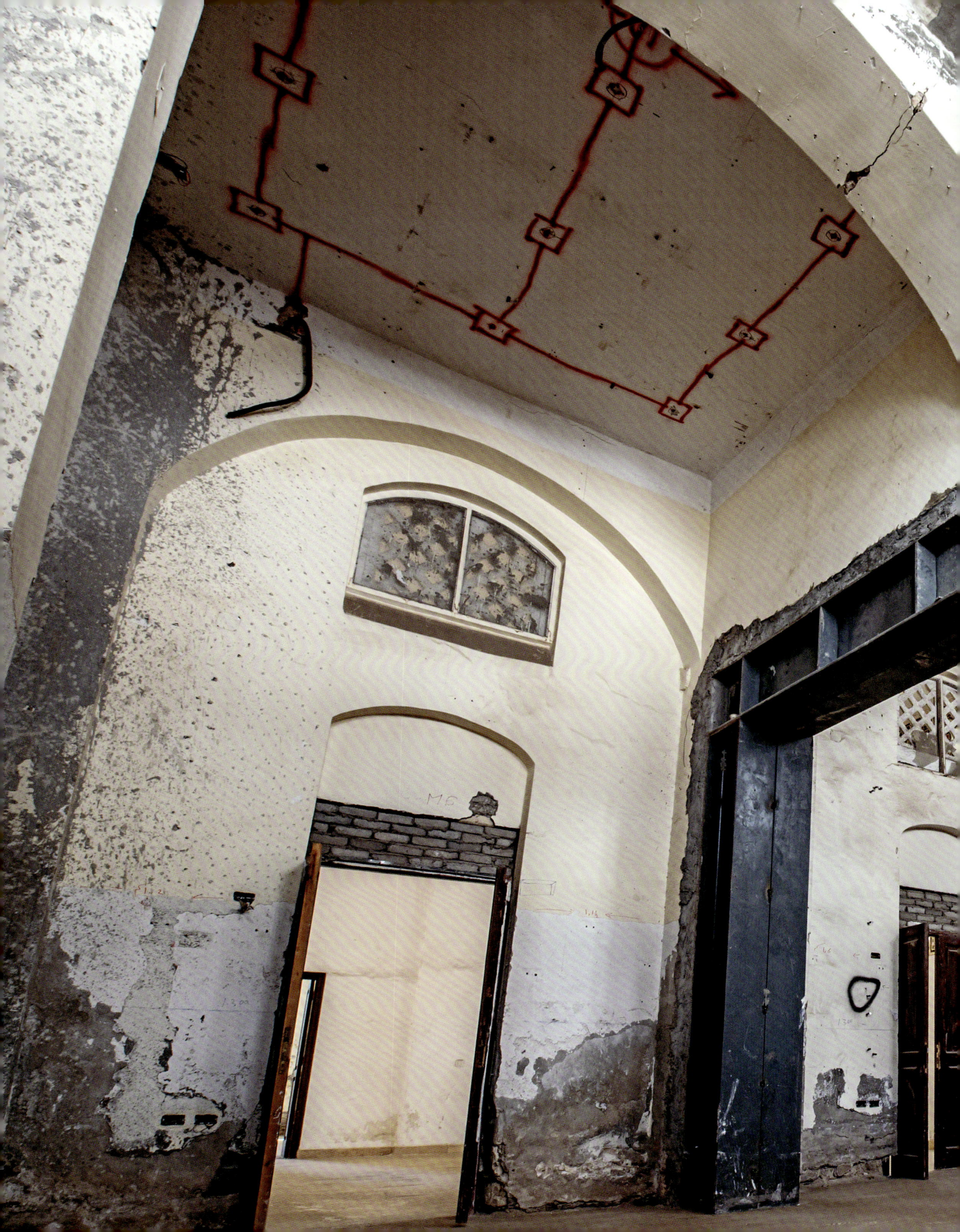

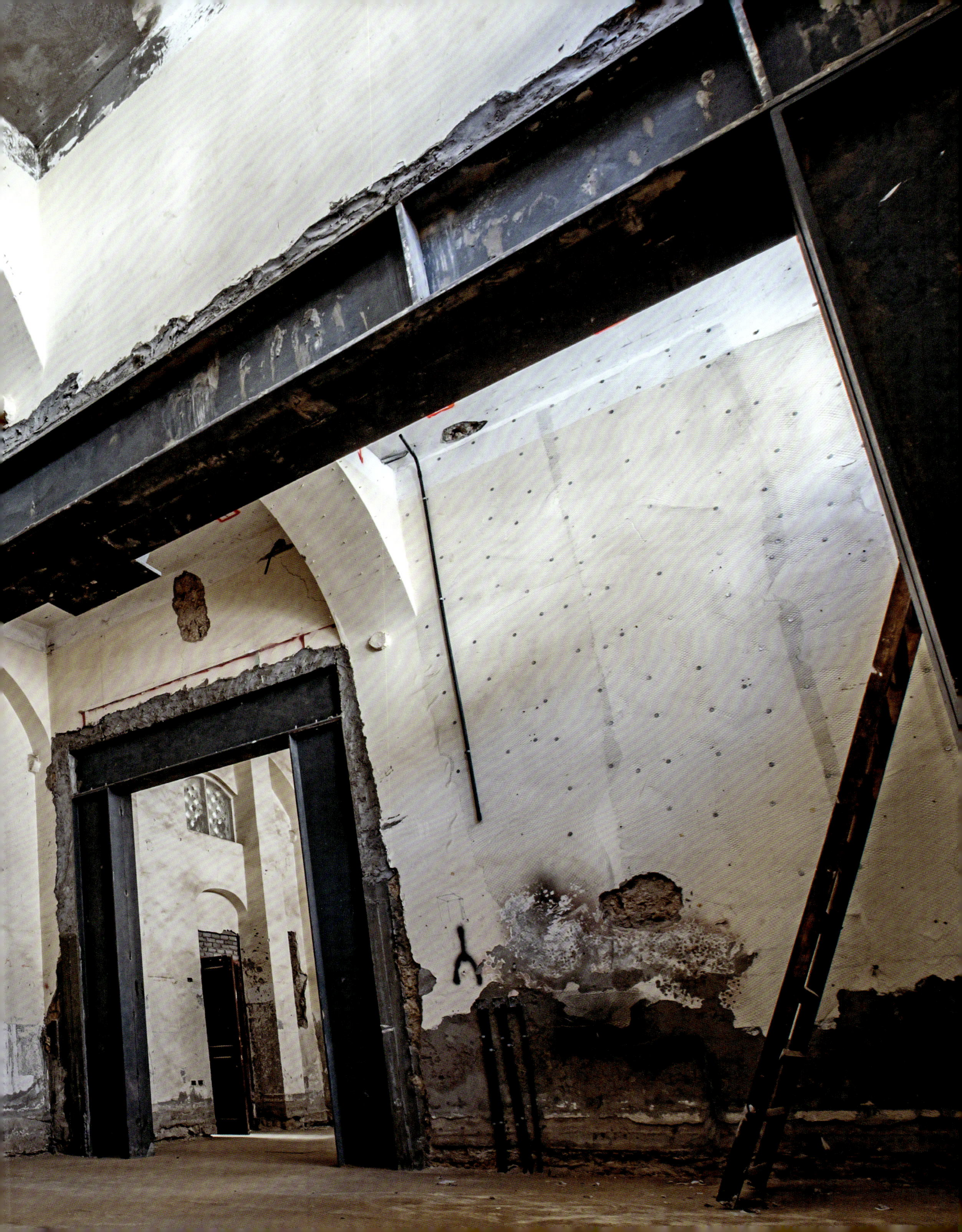

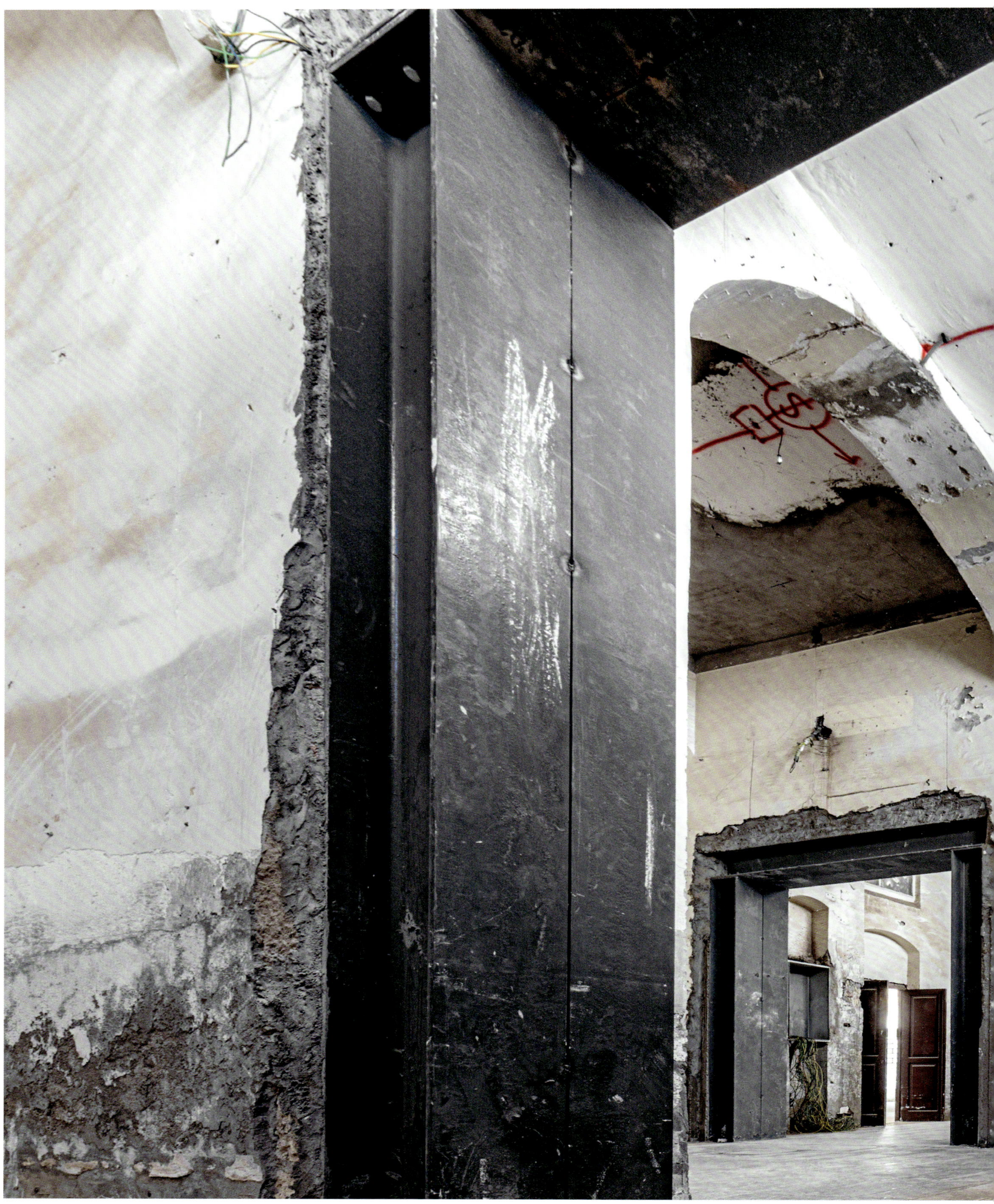

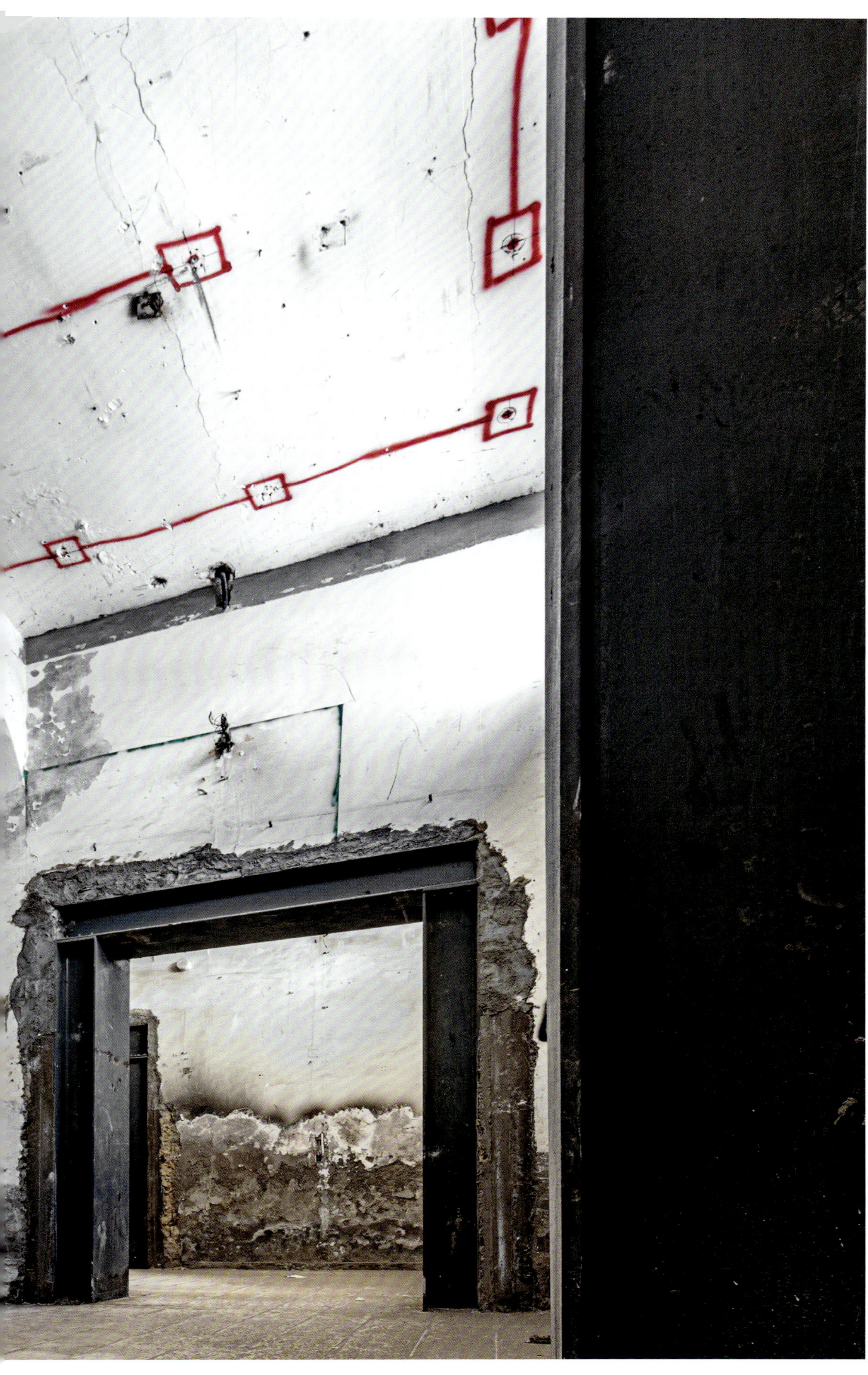

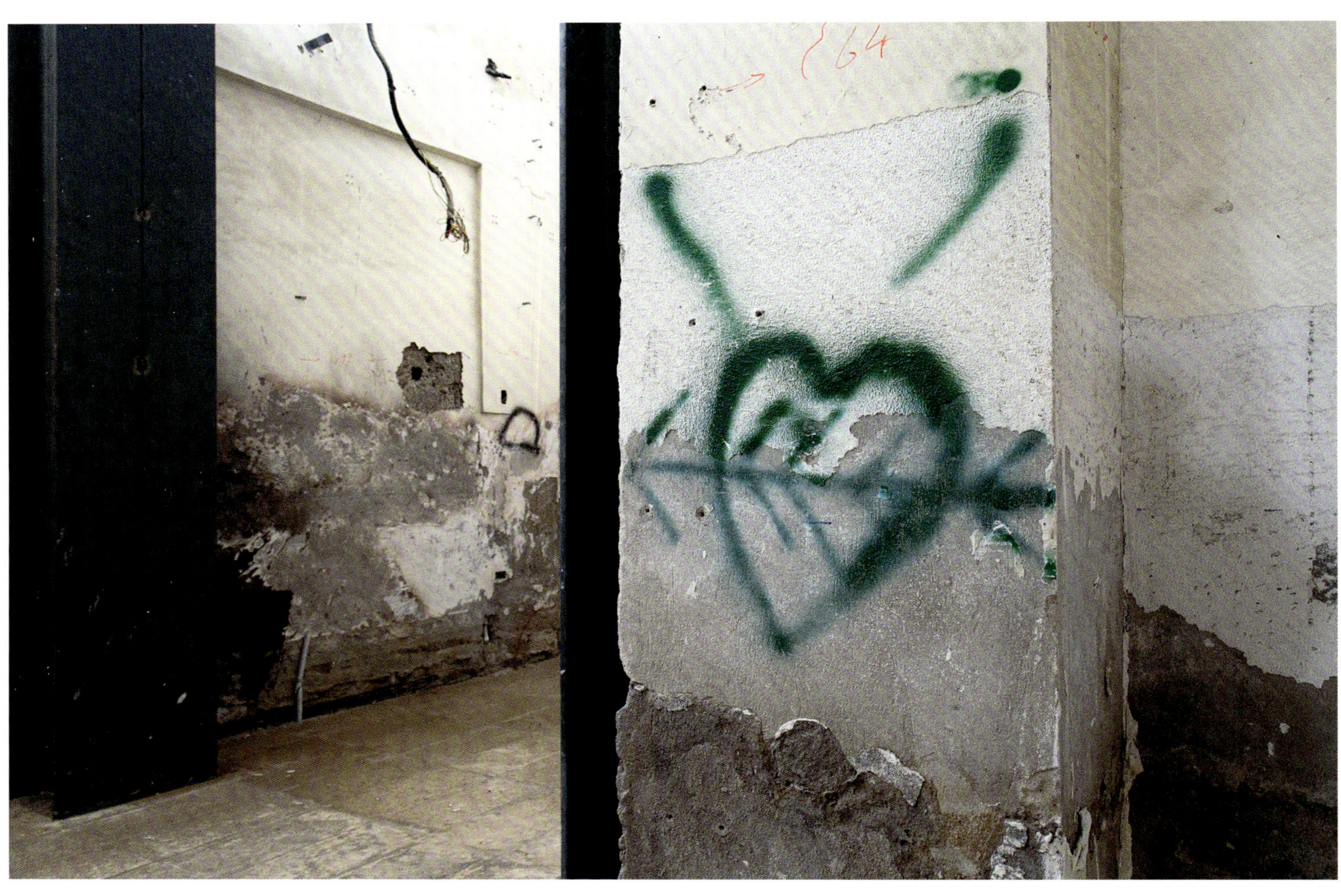

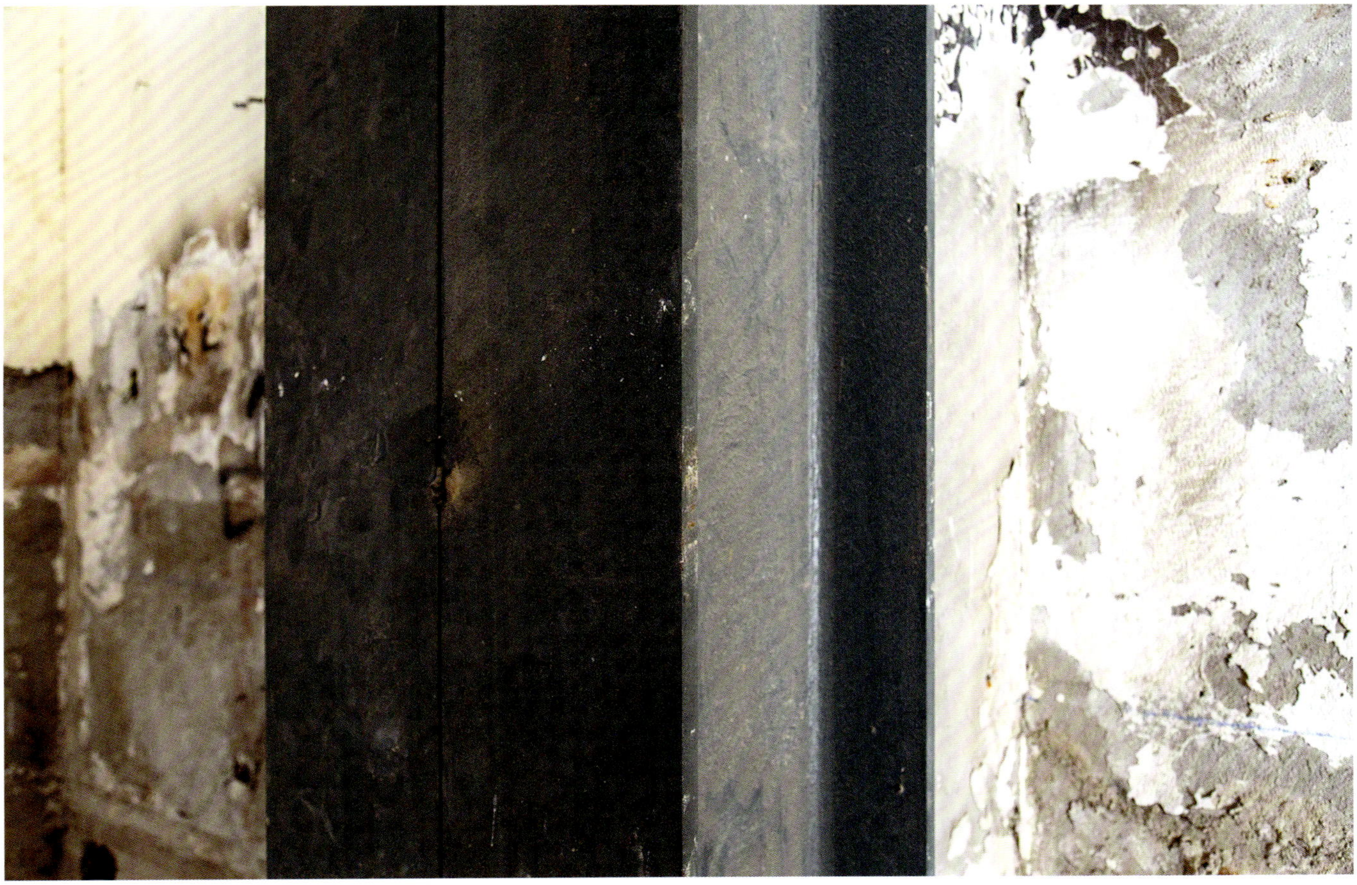

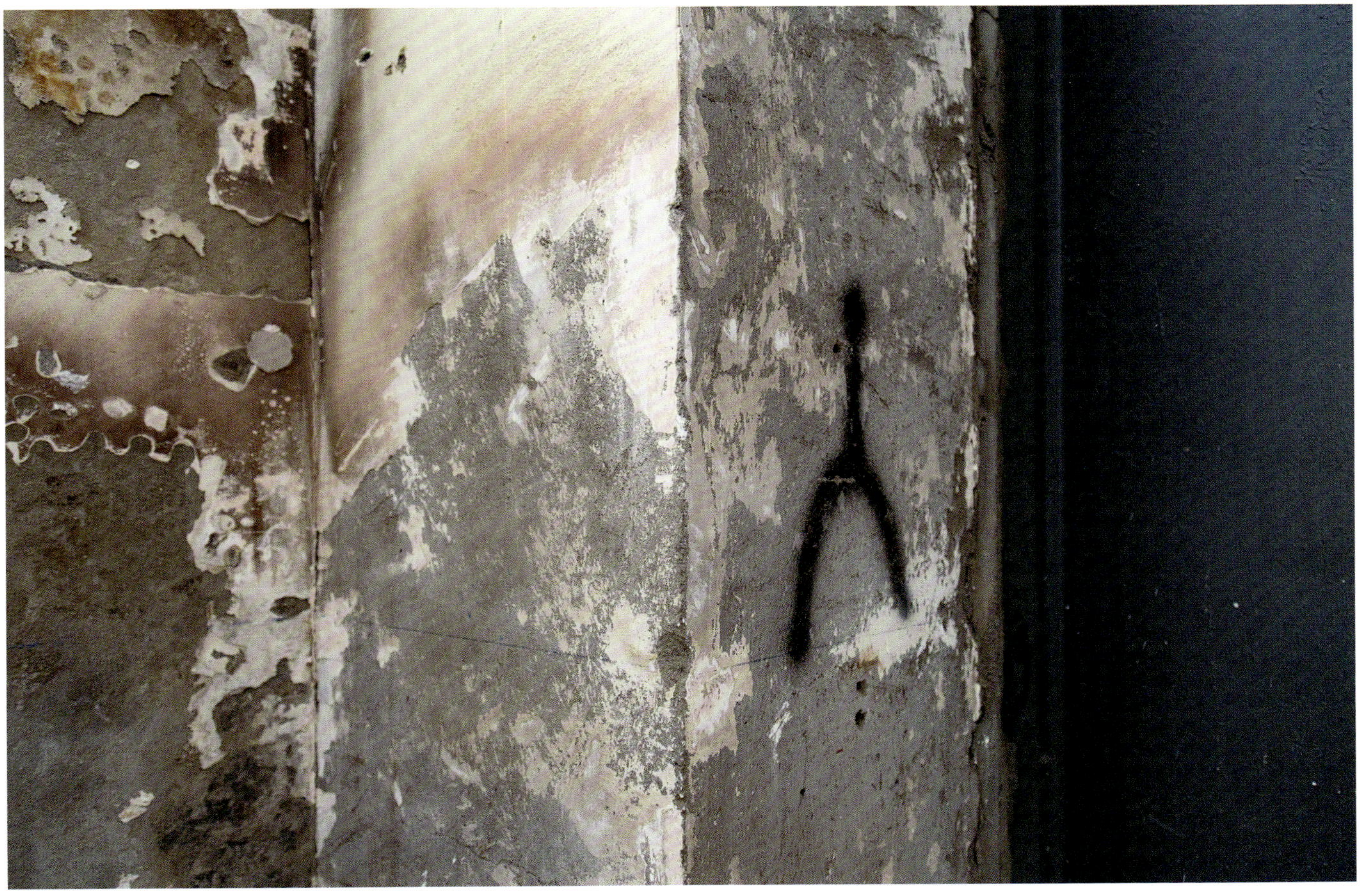

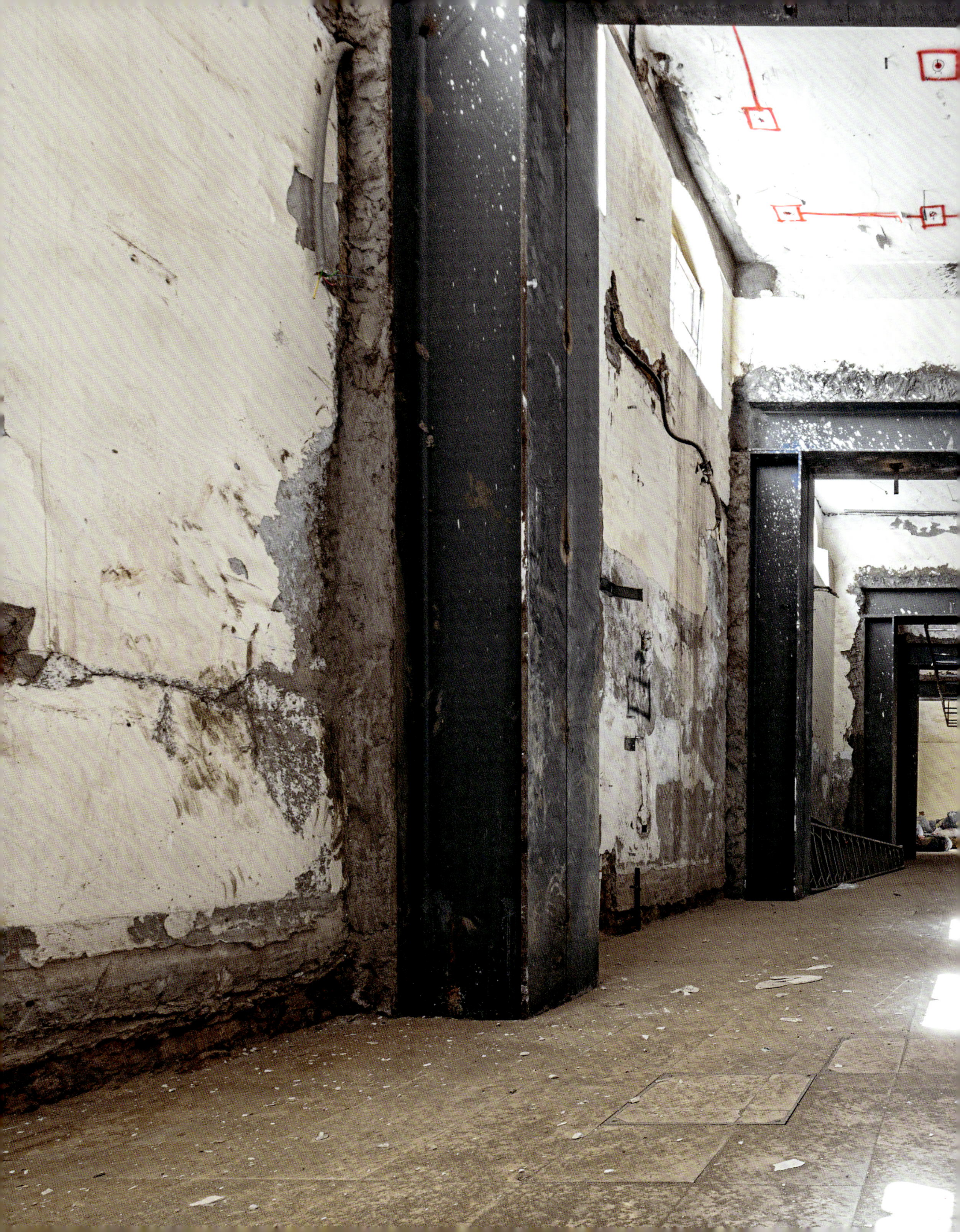

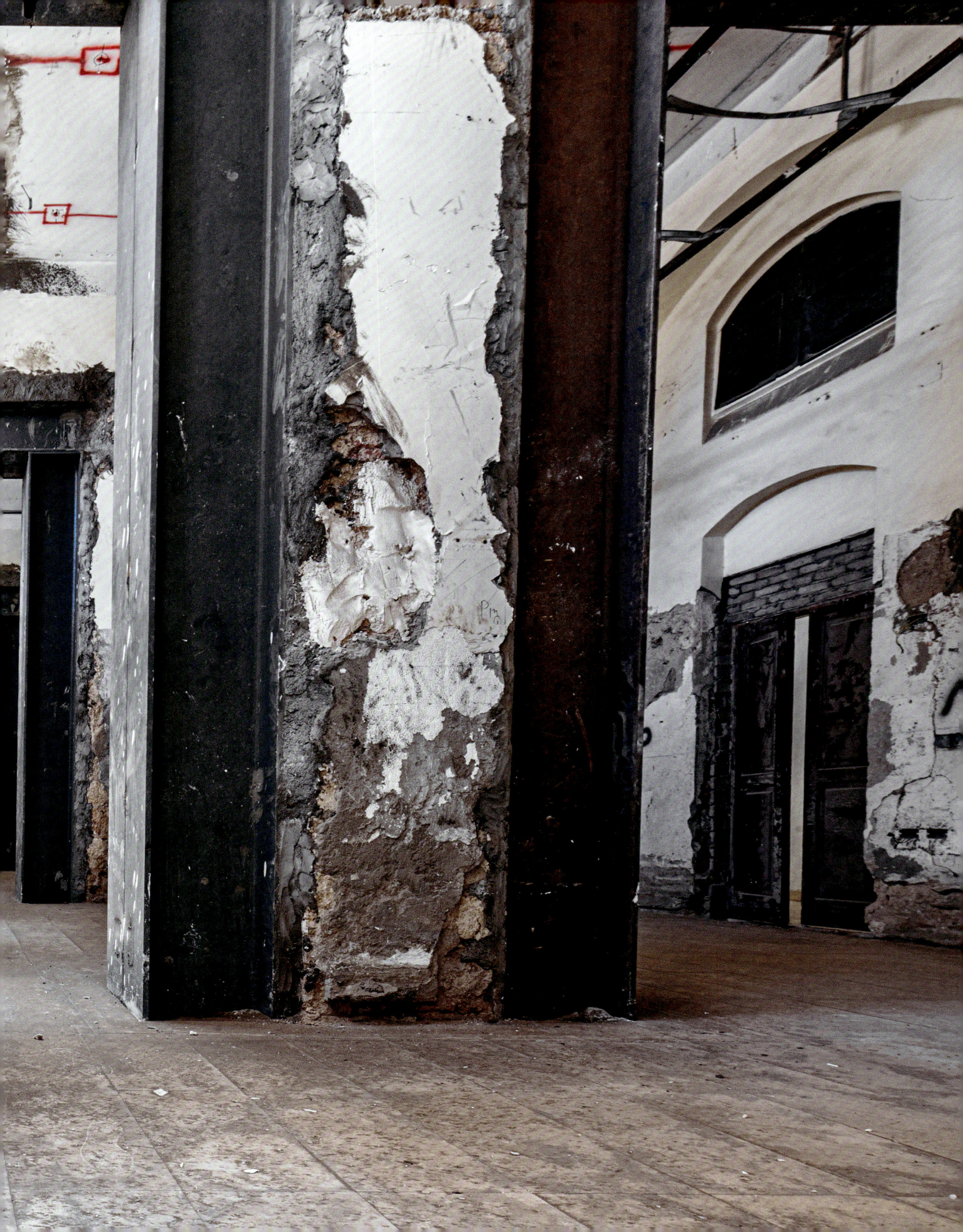

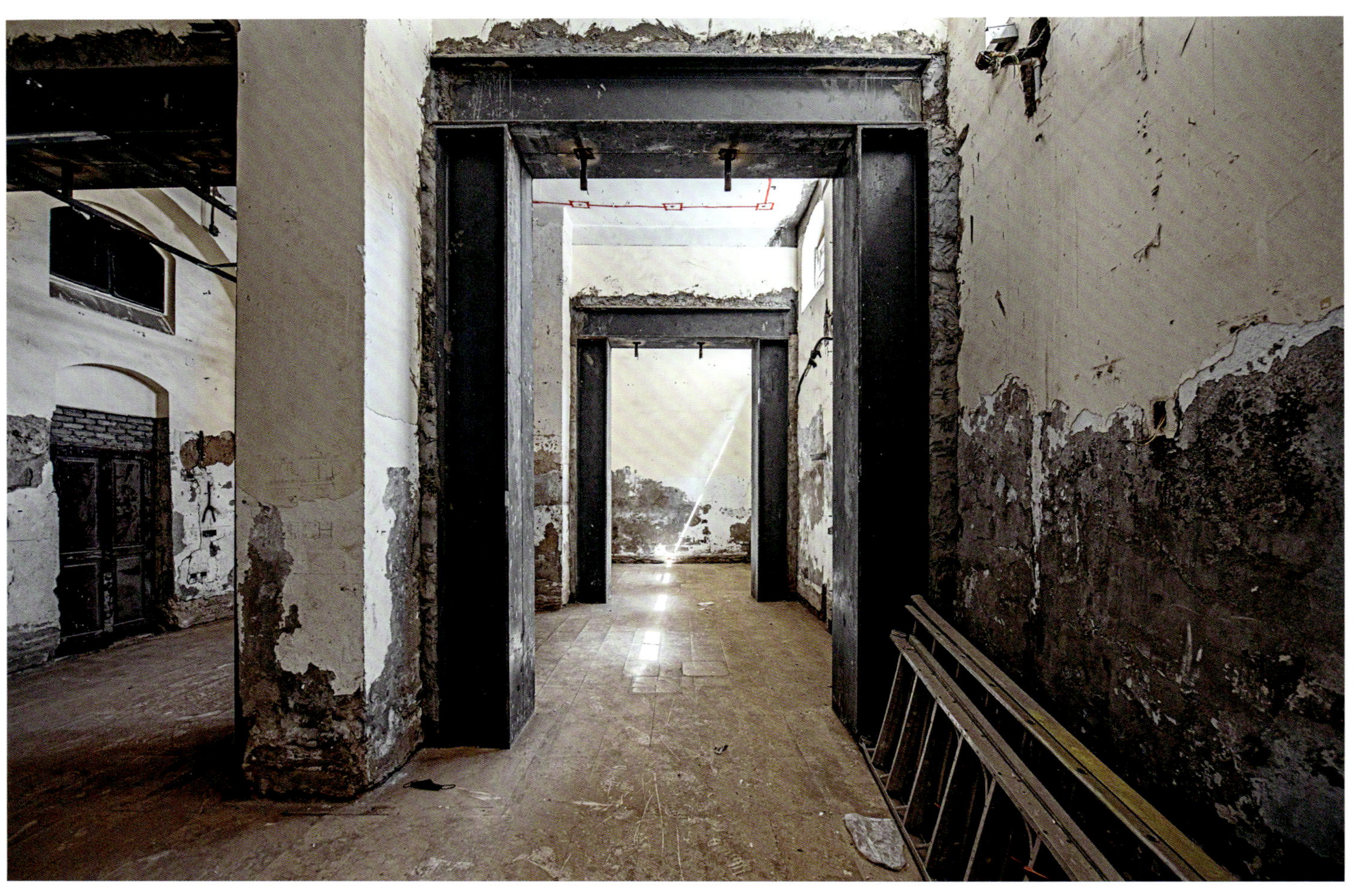

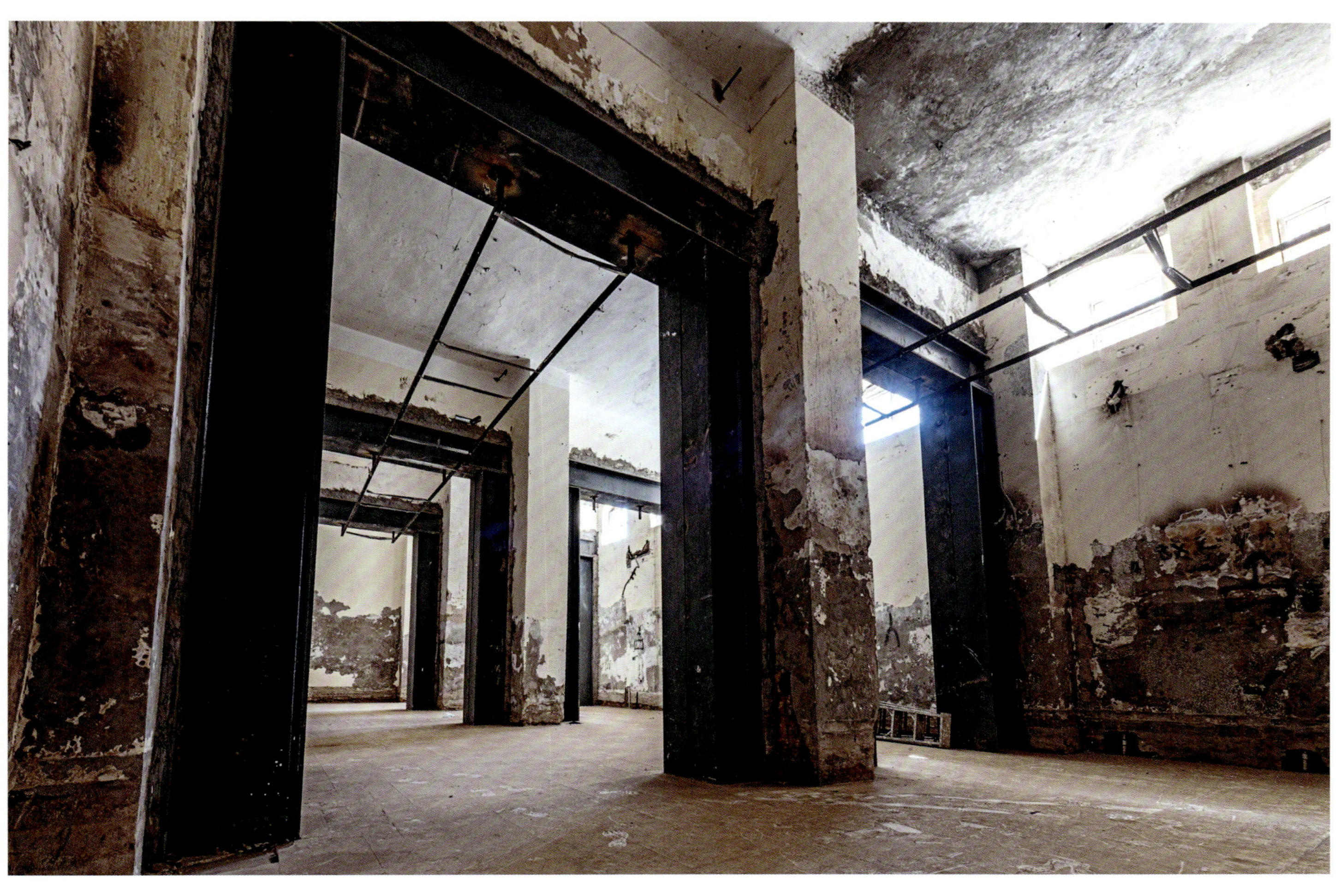

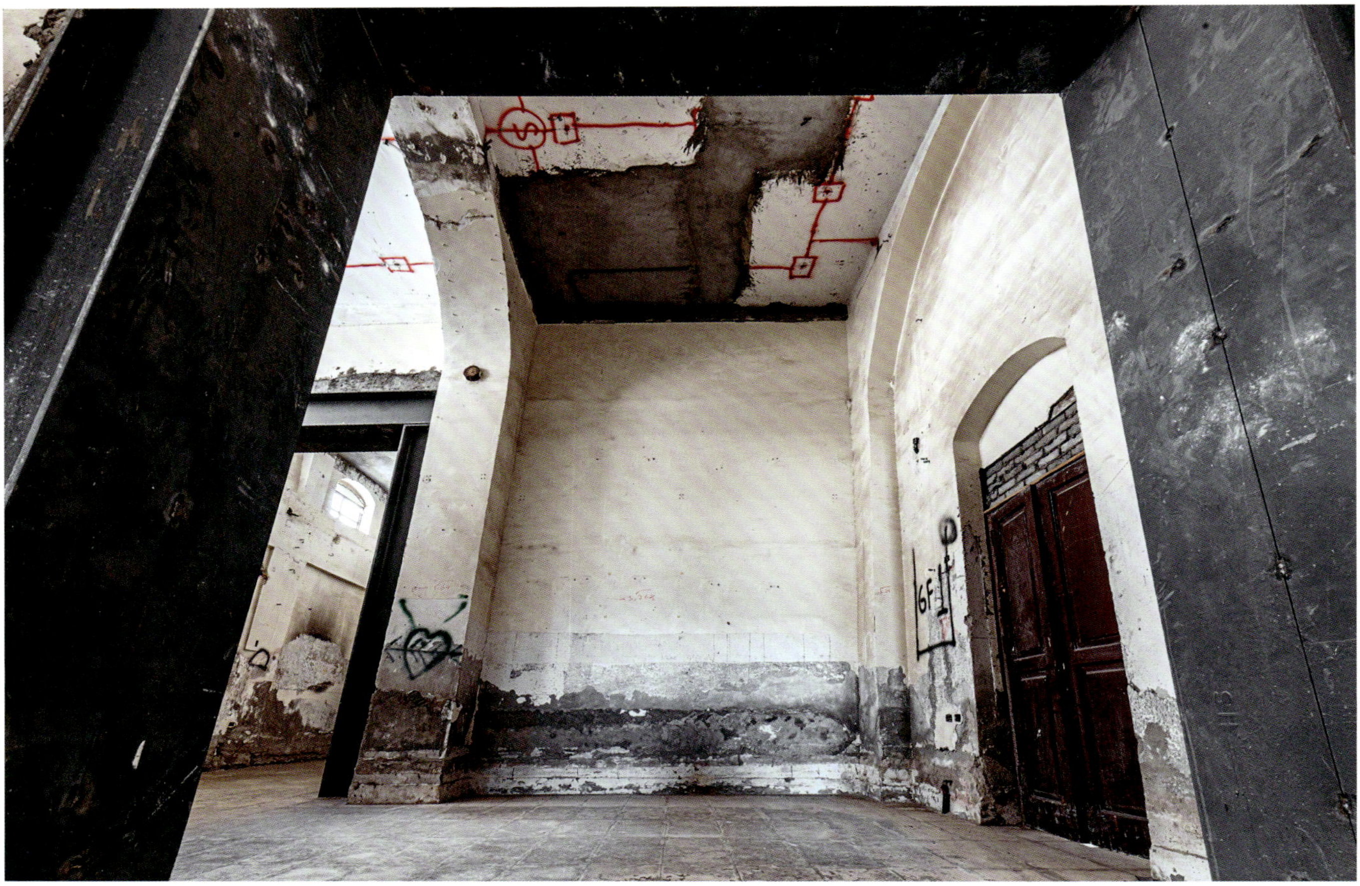

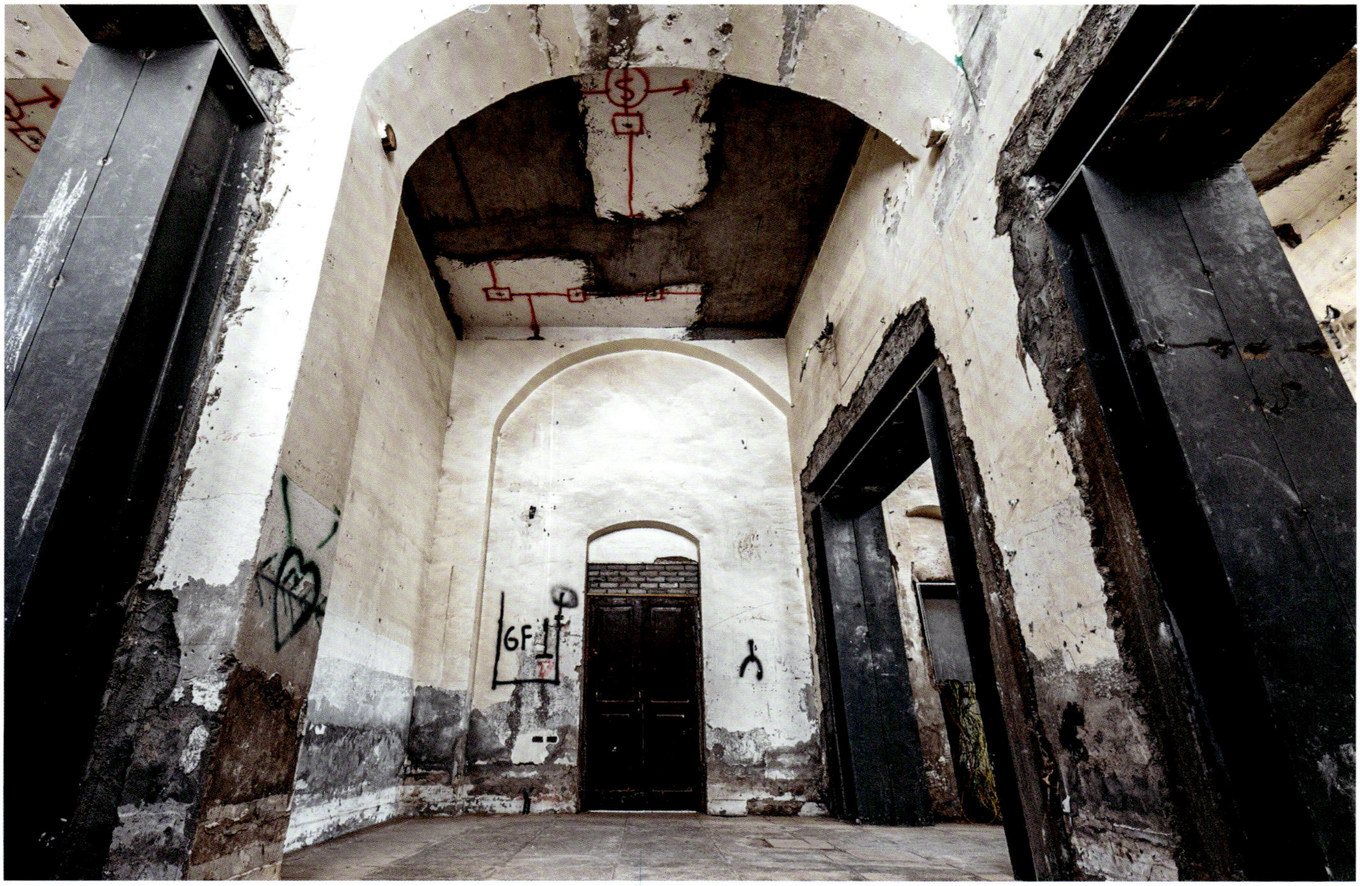

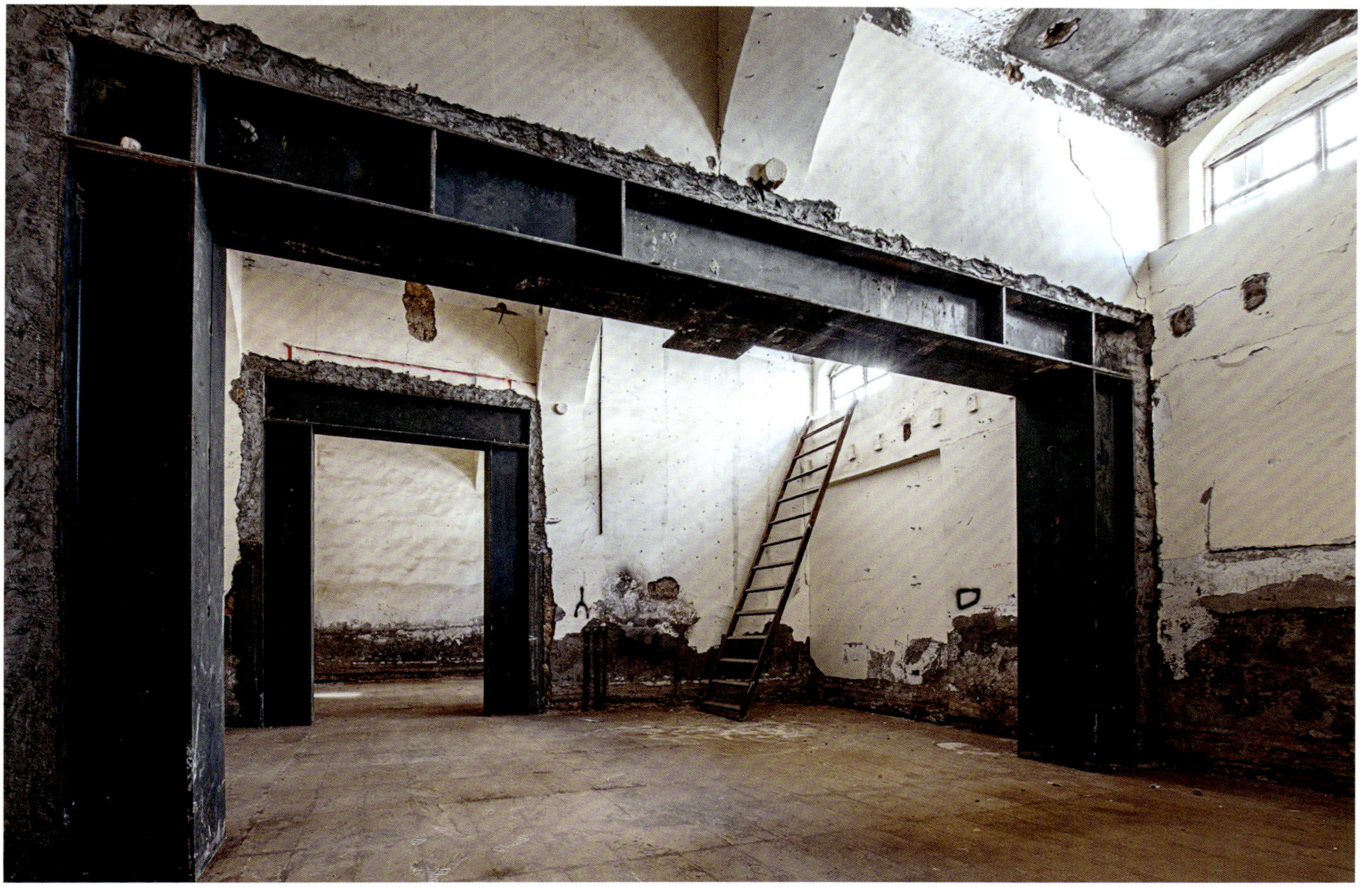

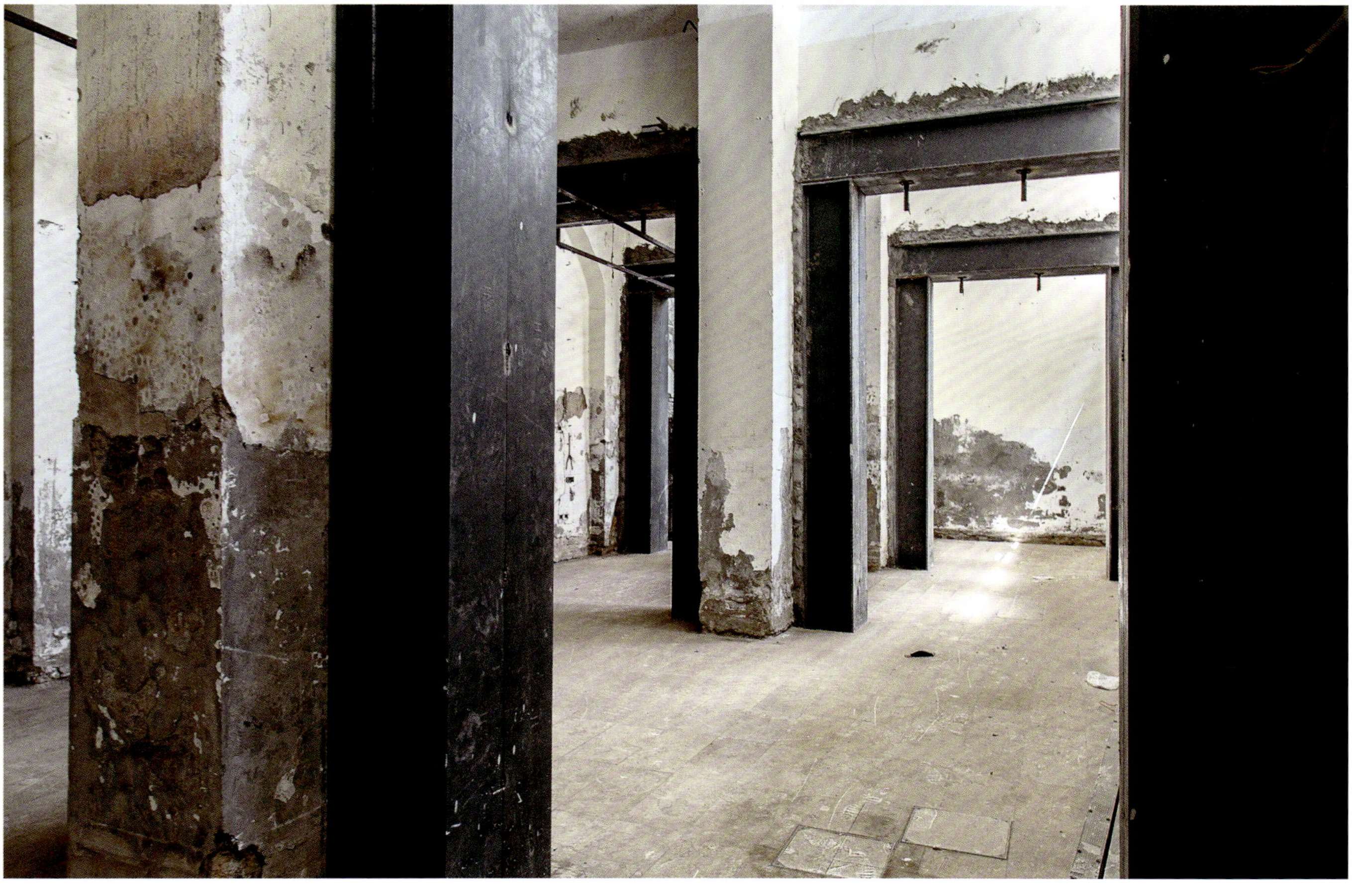

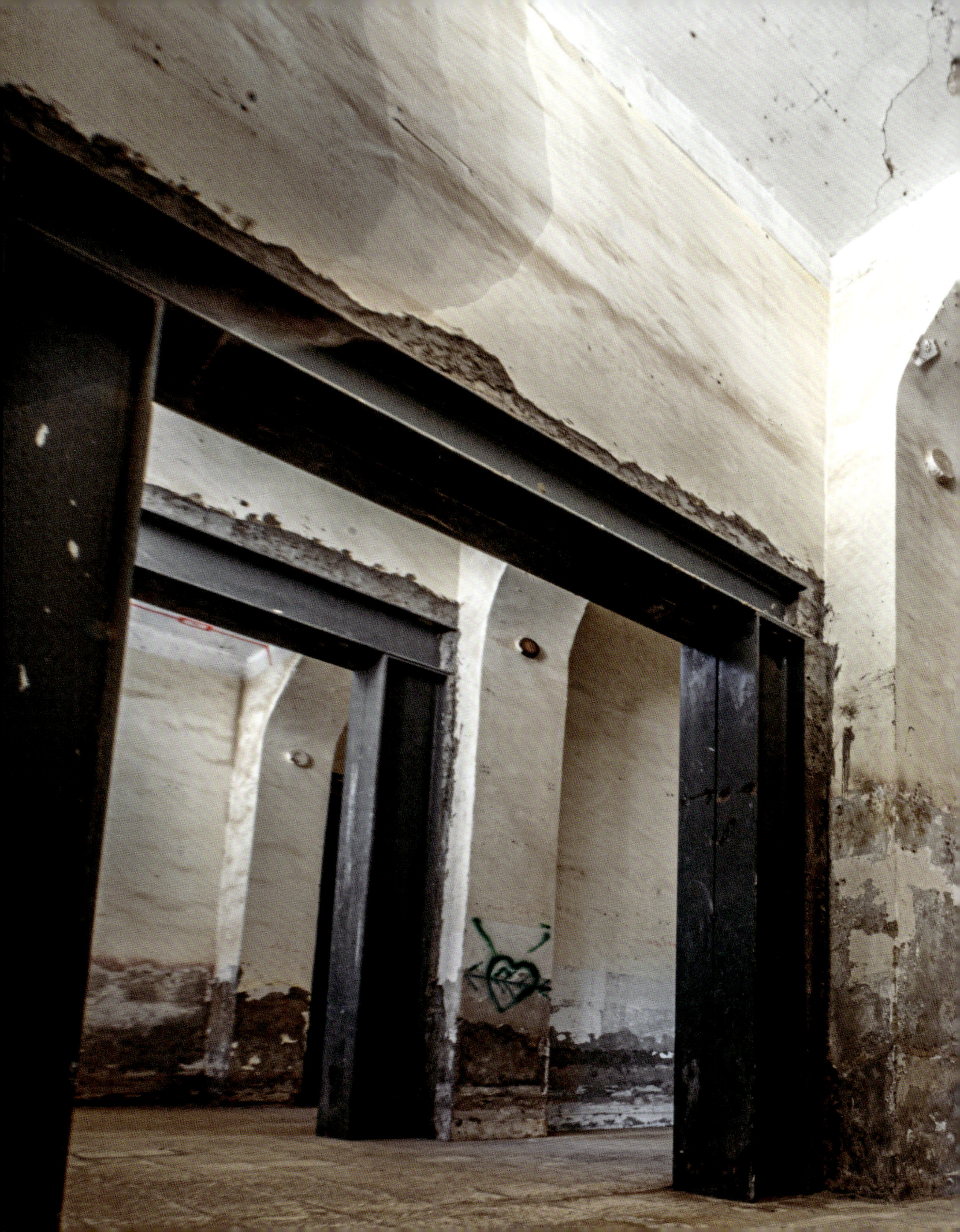

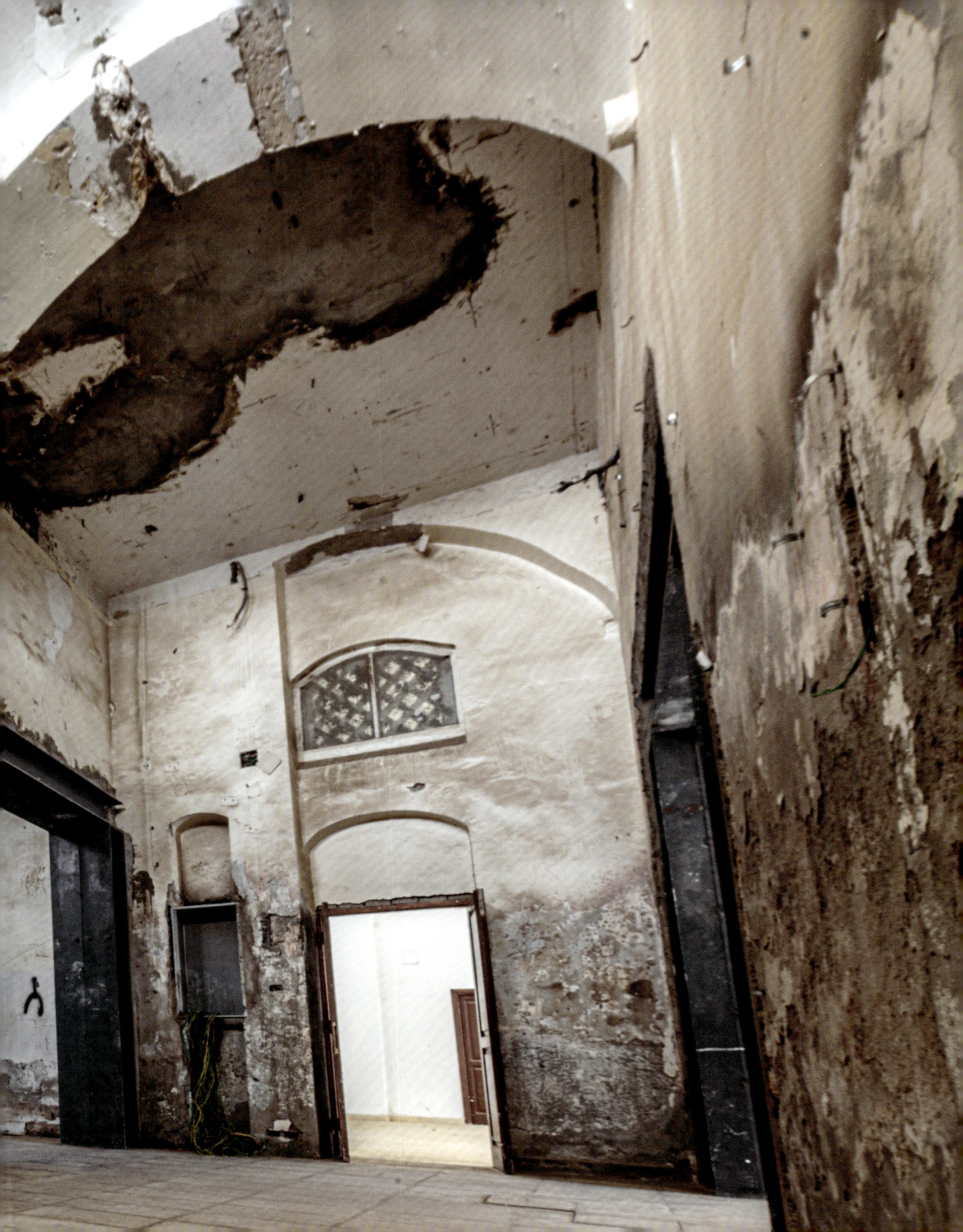

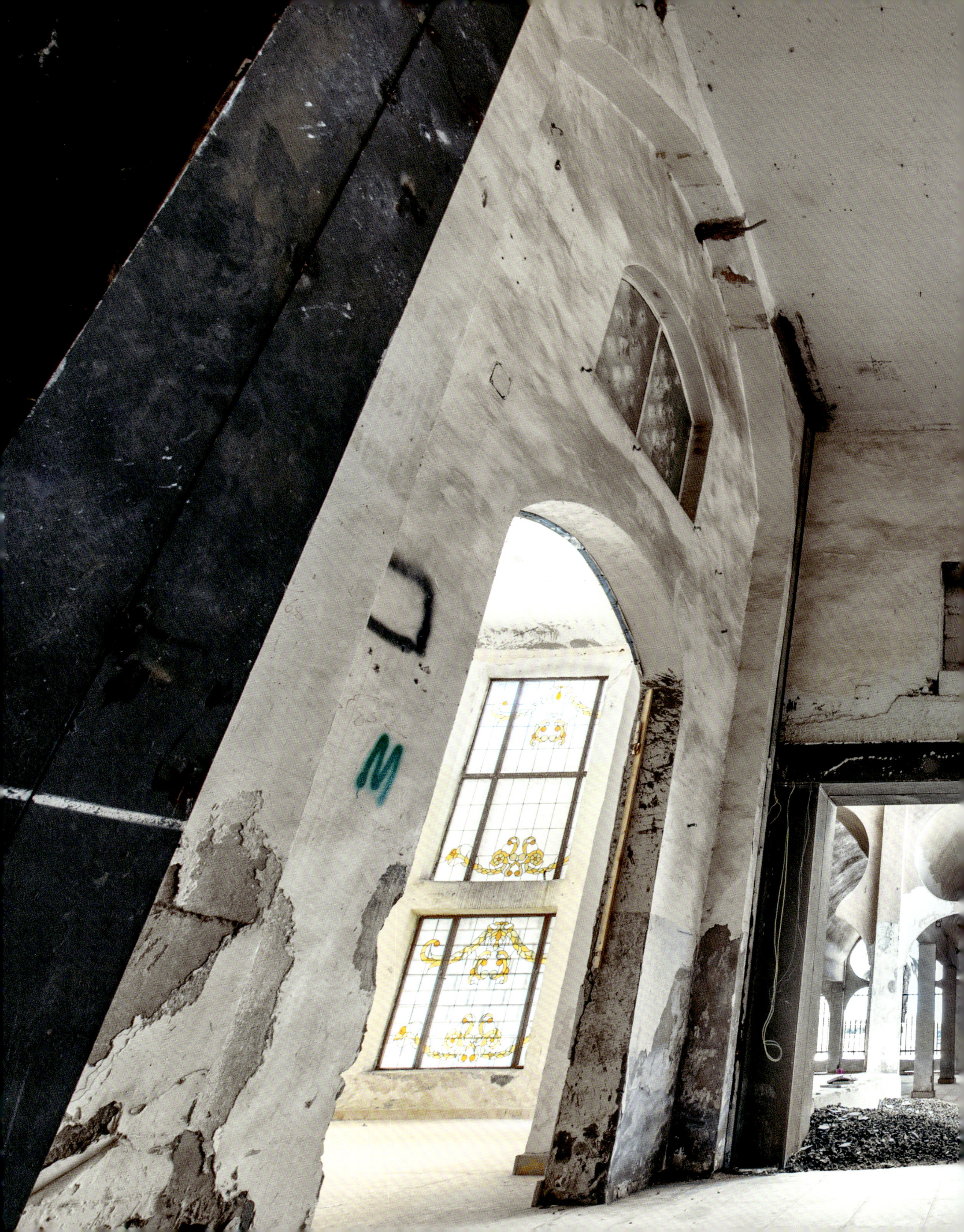

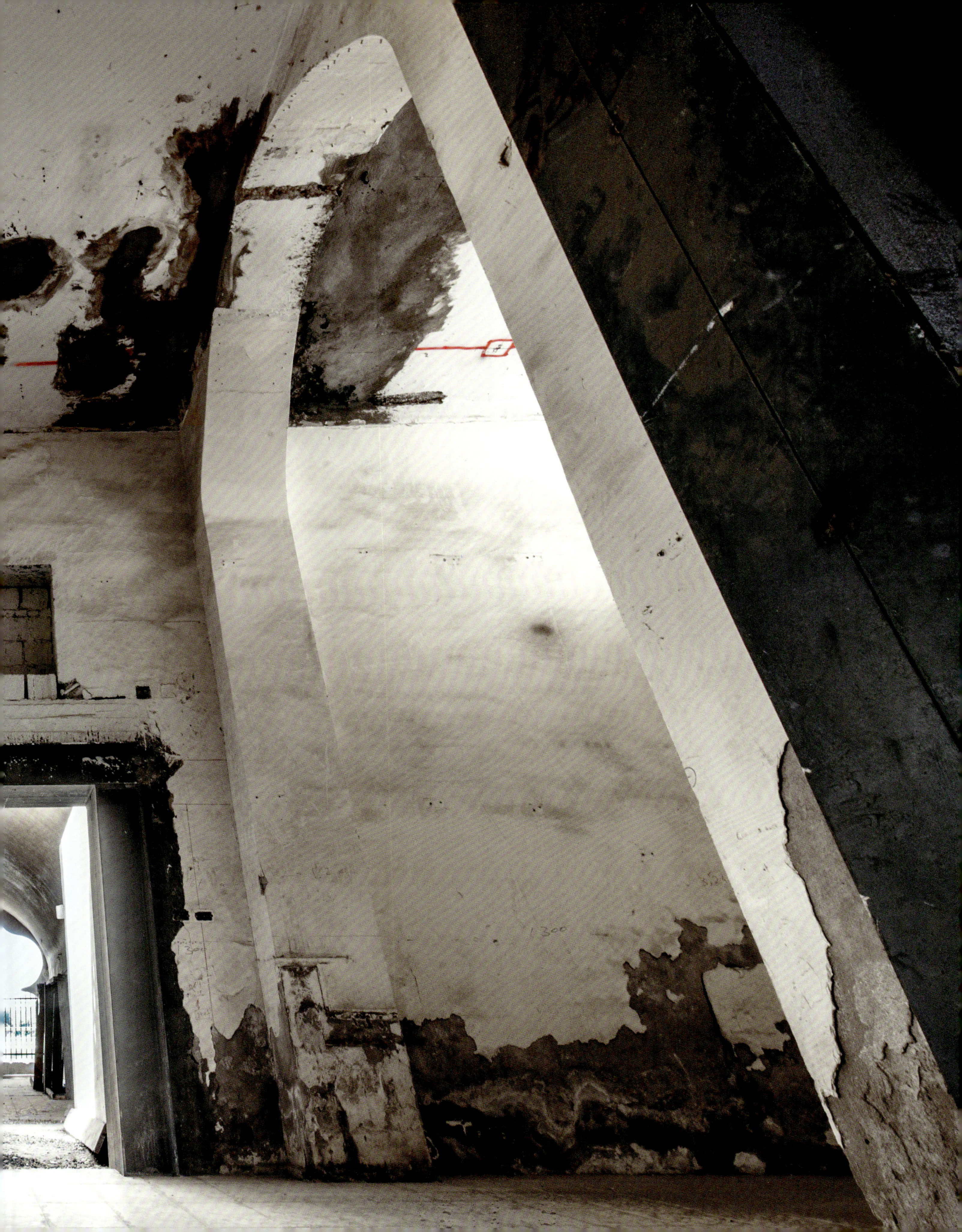

III.

On the Verge of Abstraction

It is in this way – through these signs, marks, and traces that may seem minuscule – that, on the verge of abstraction, a kind of geography or cosmography is set up, in the maze of which Moath Alofi invites us to follow him.

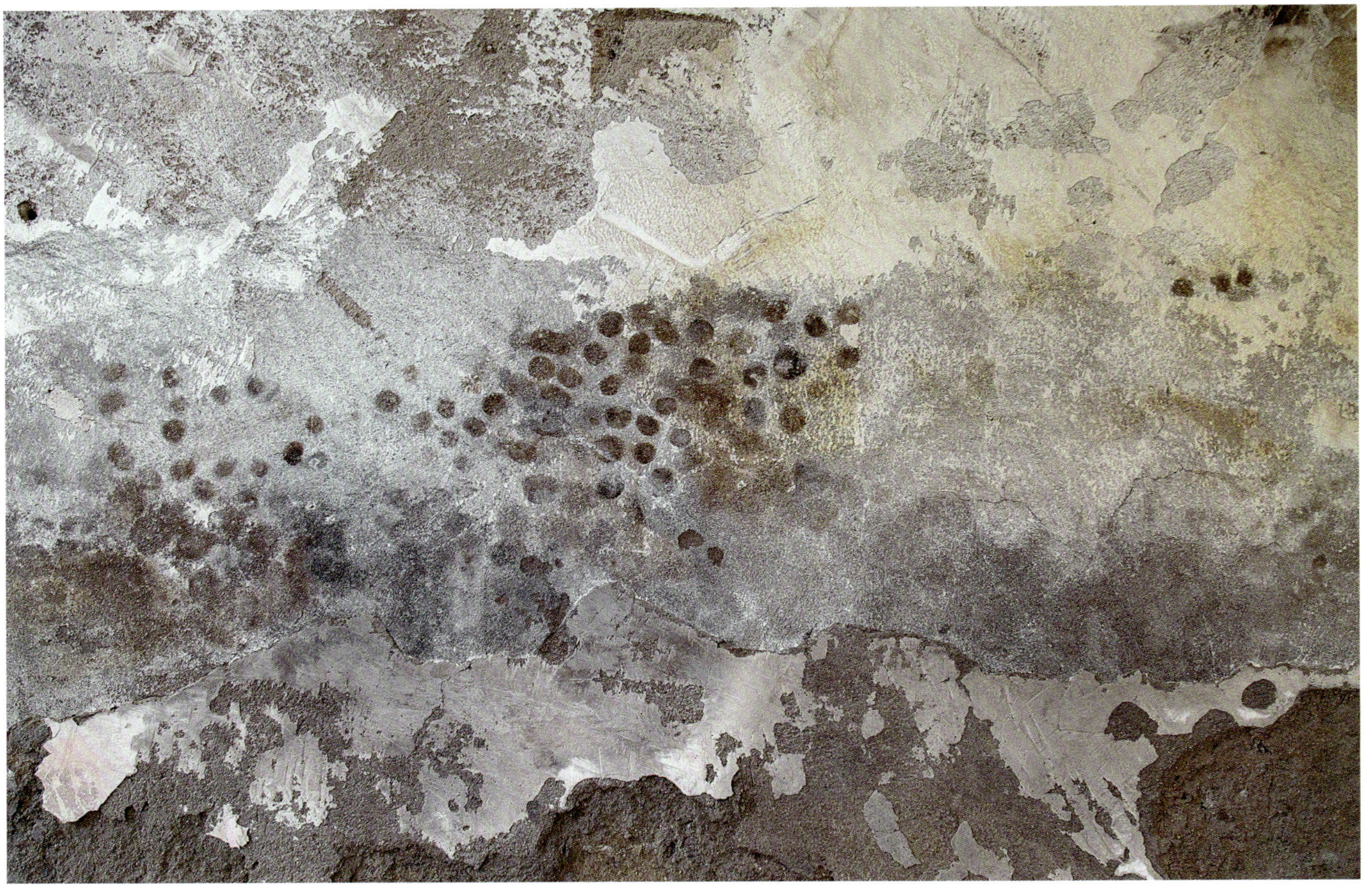

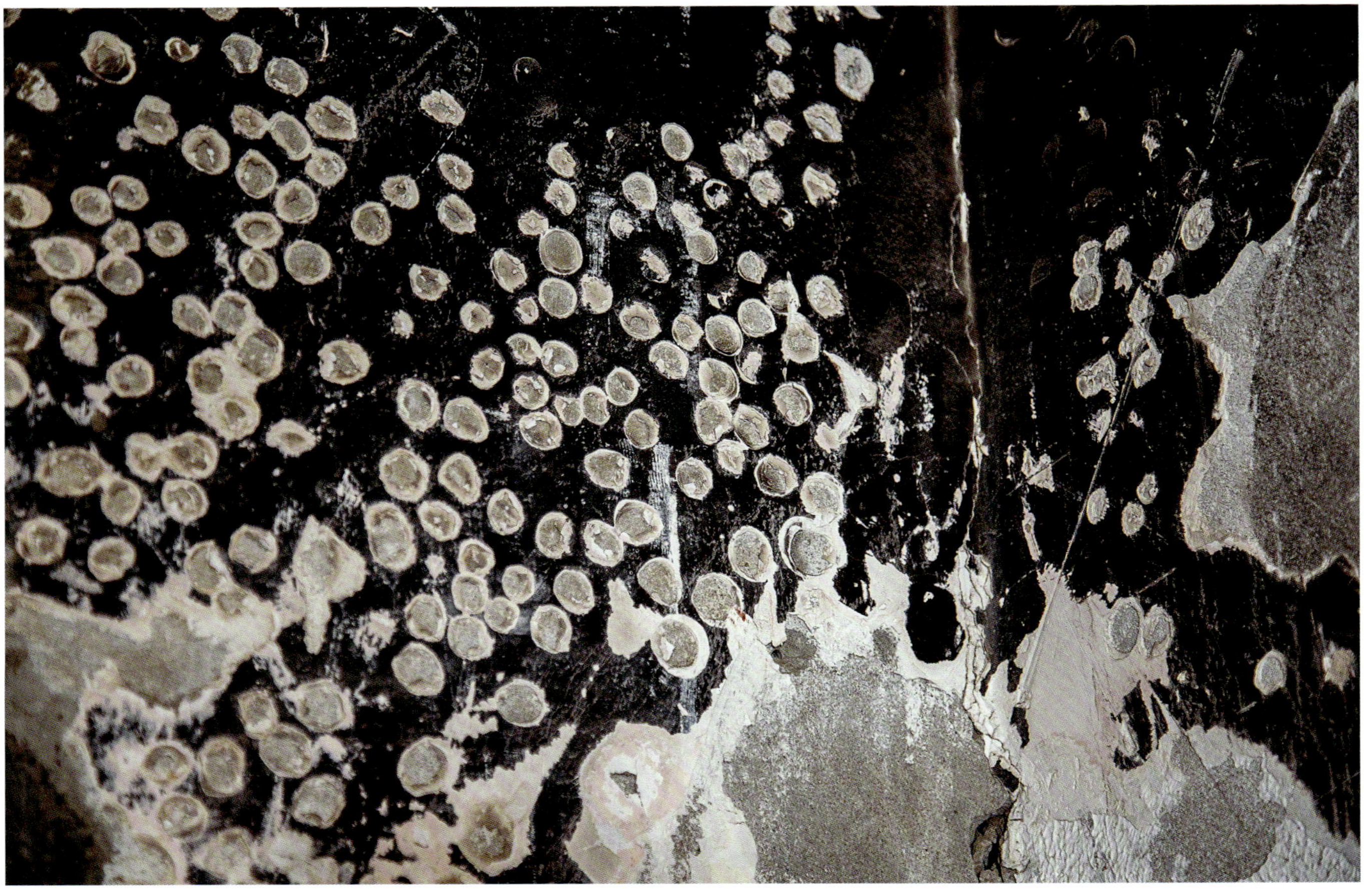

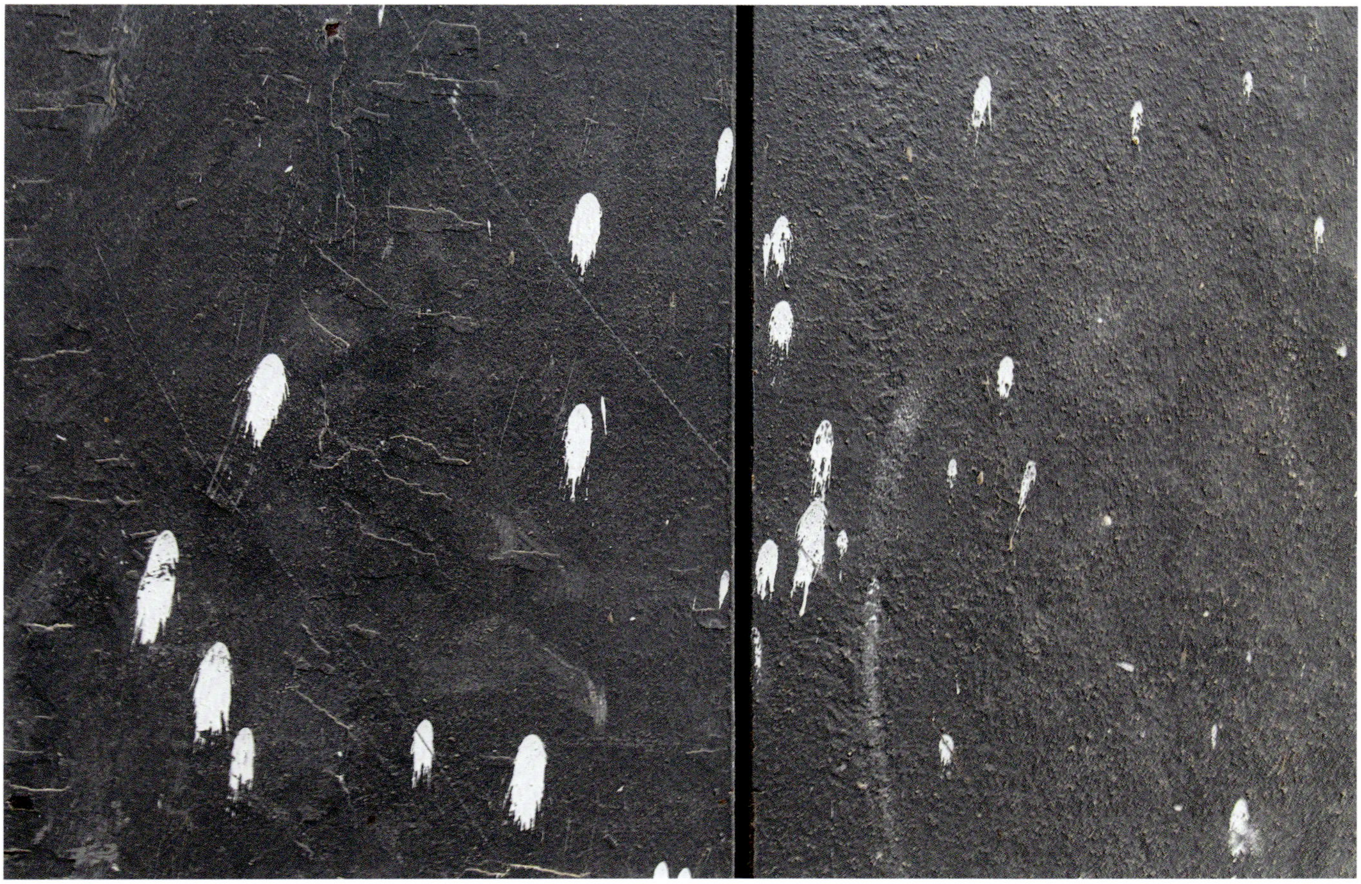

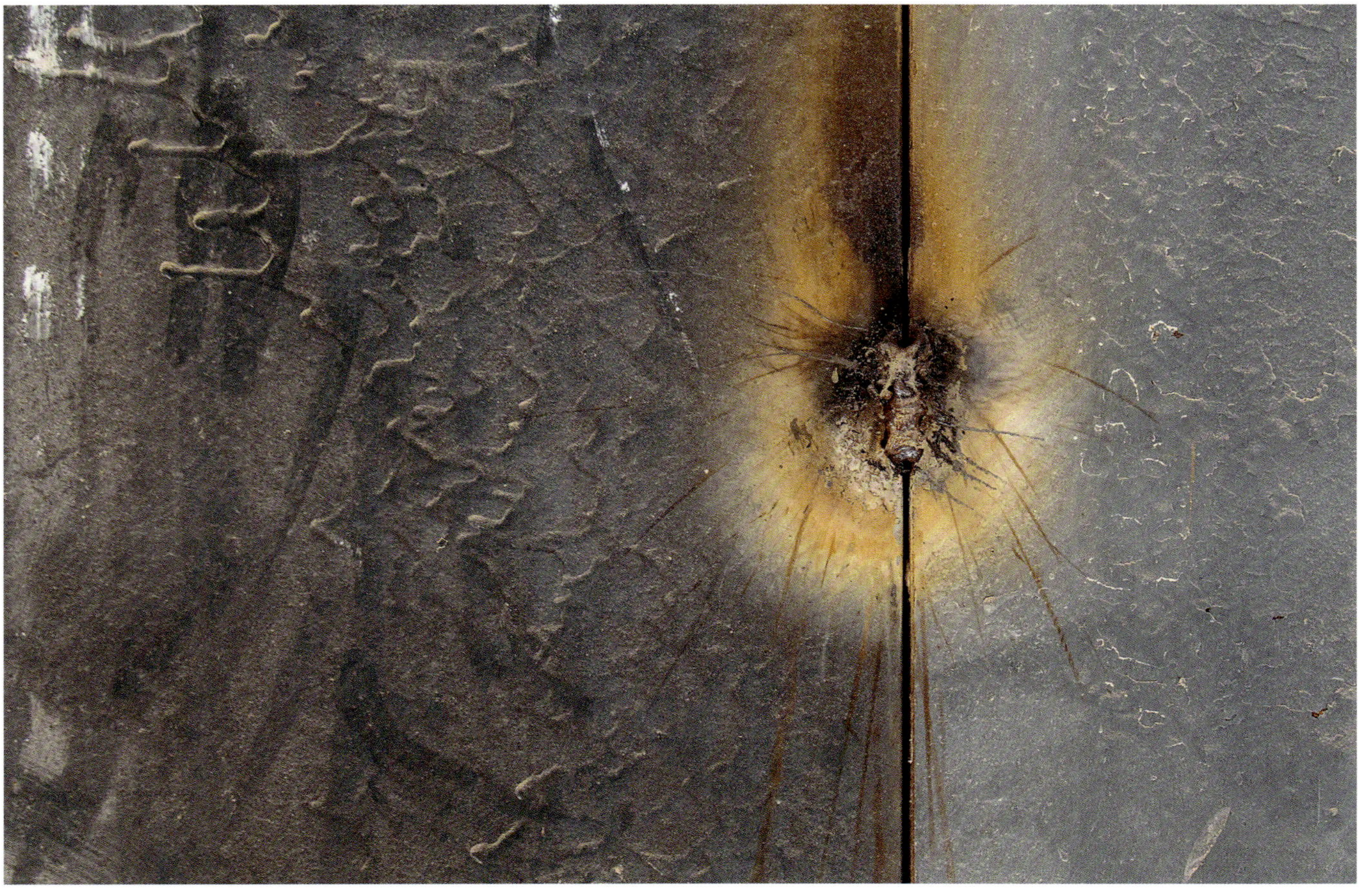

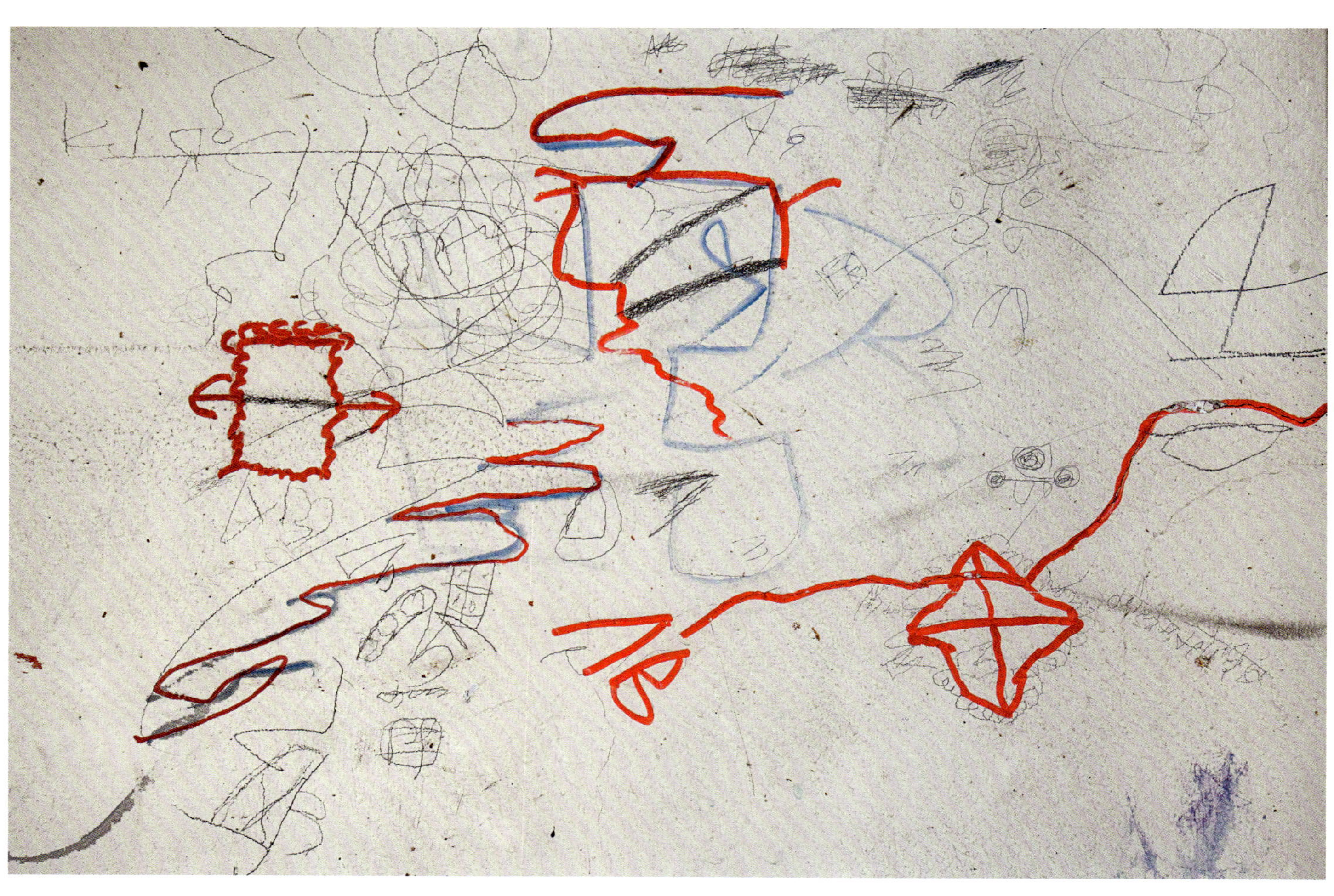

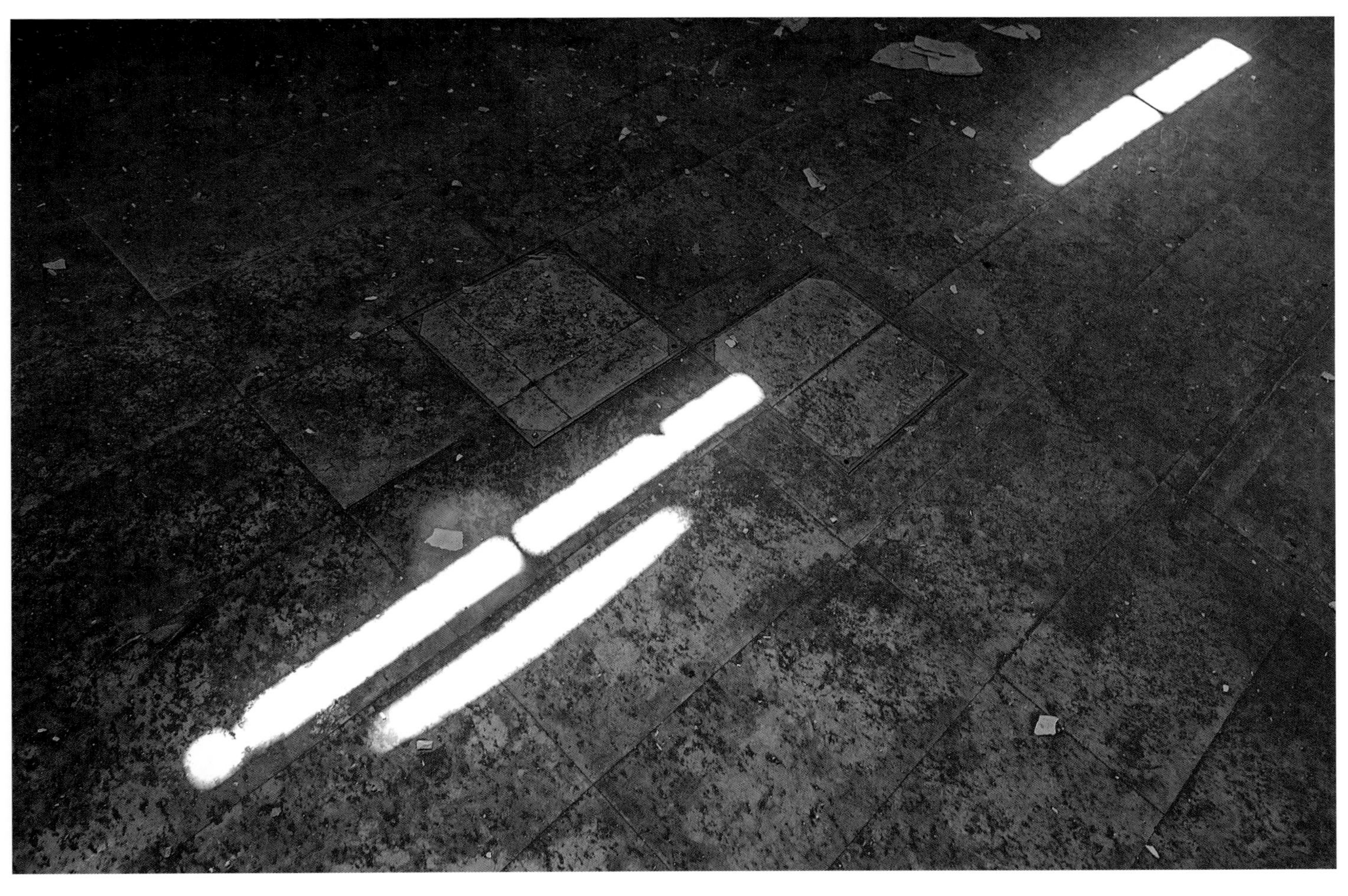

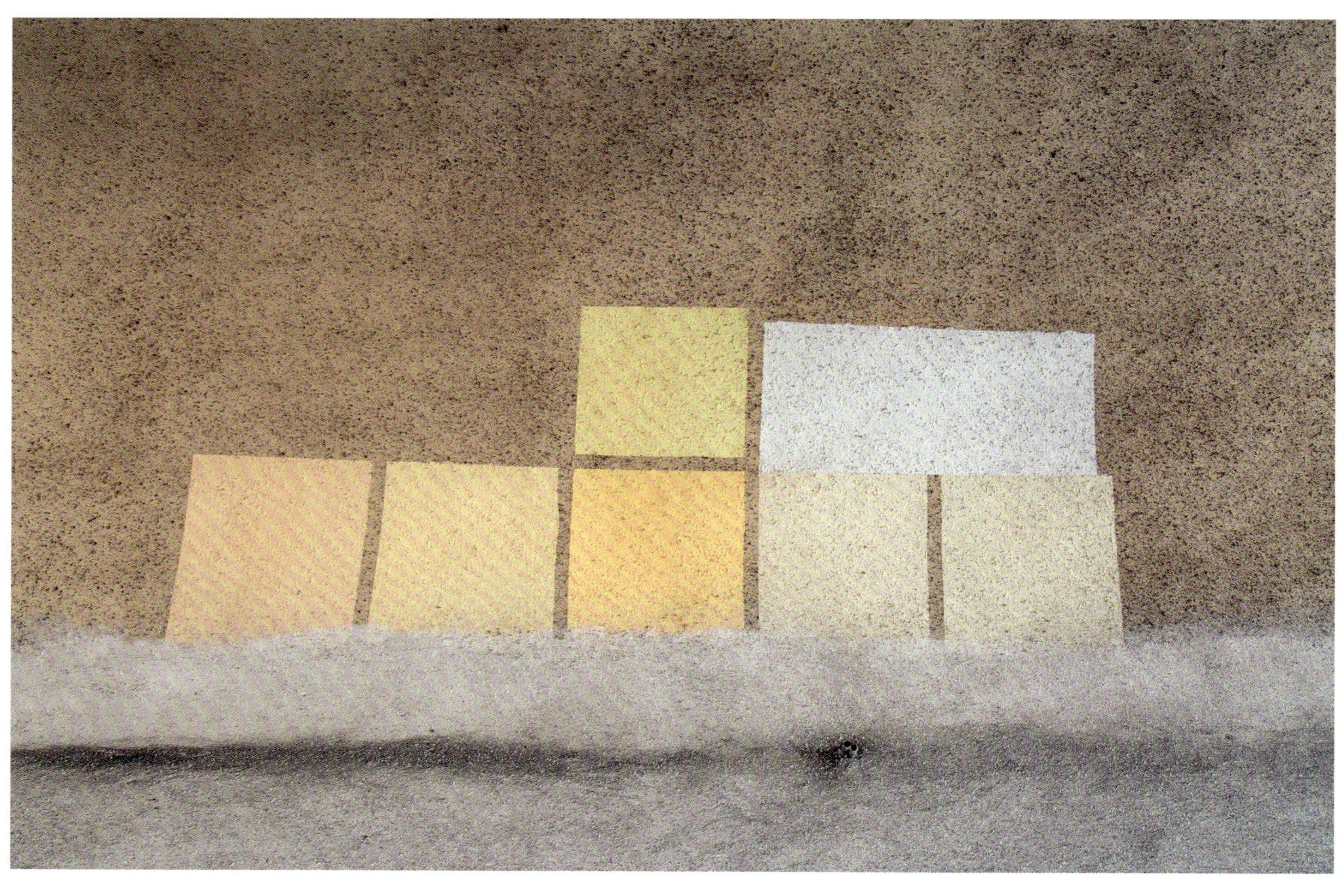

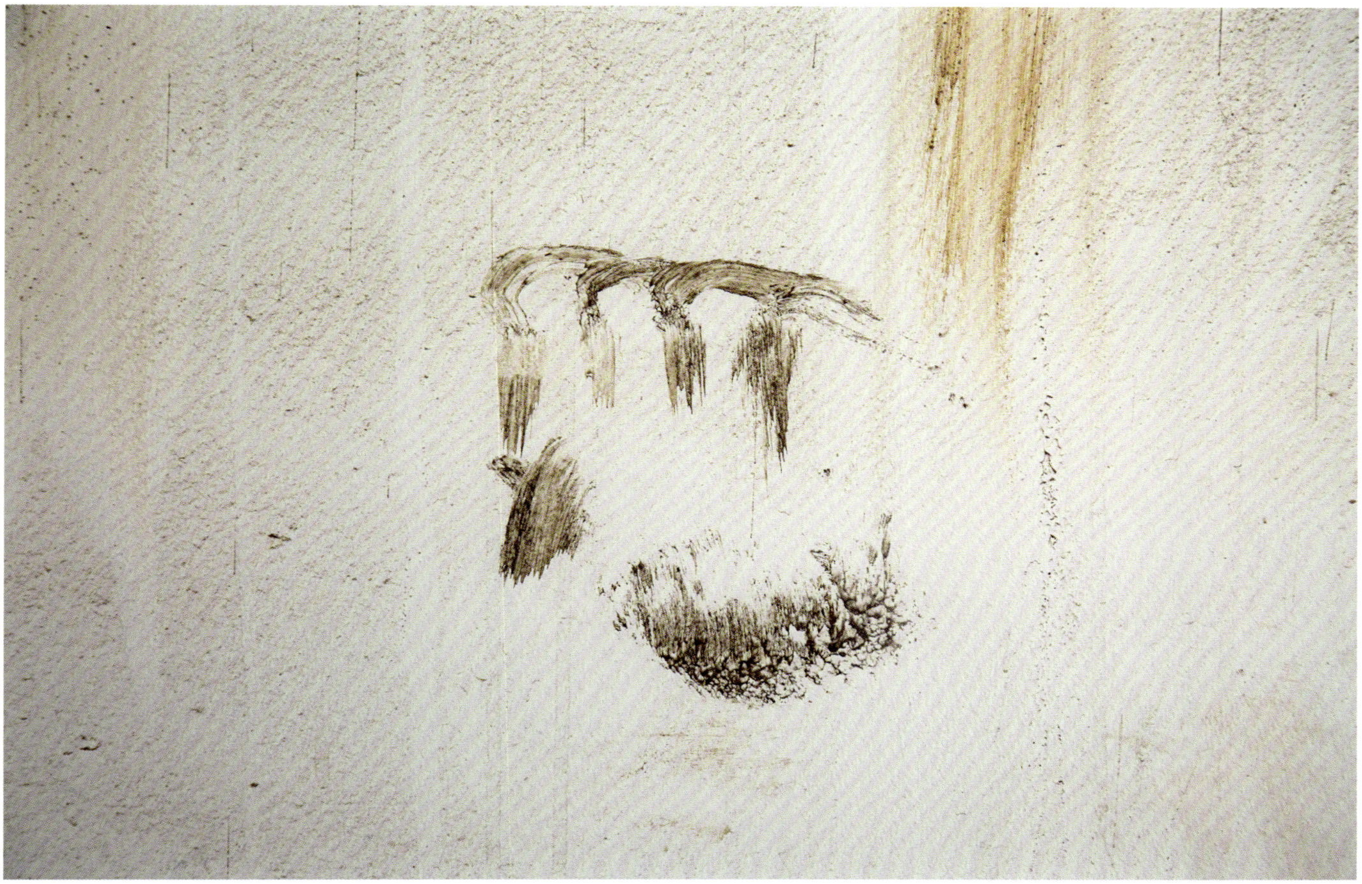

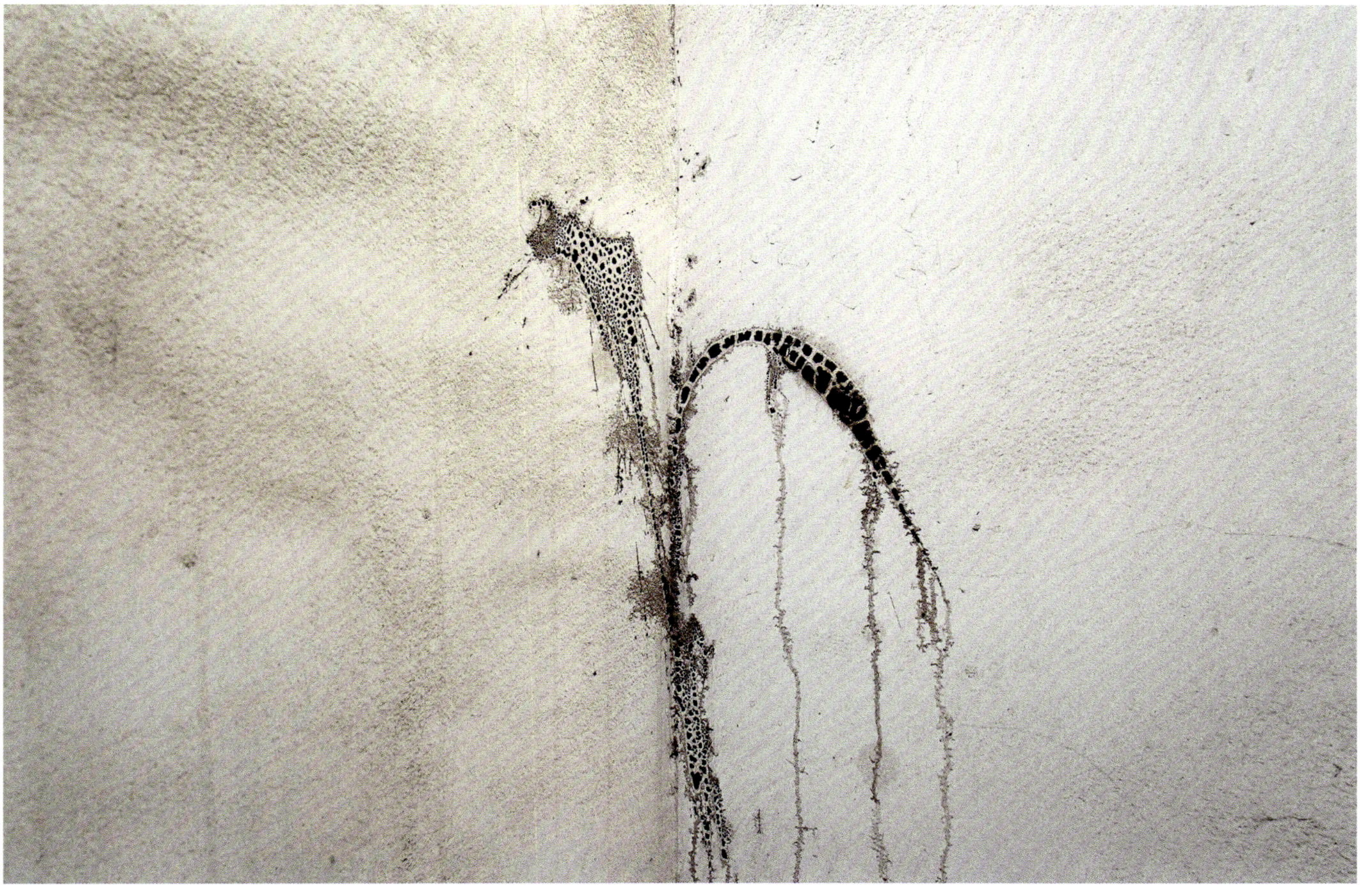

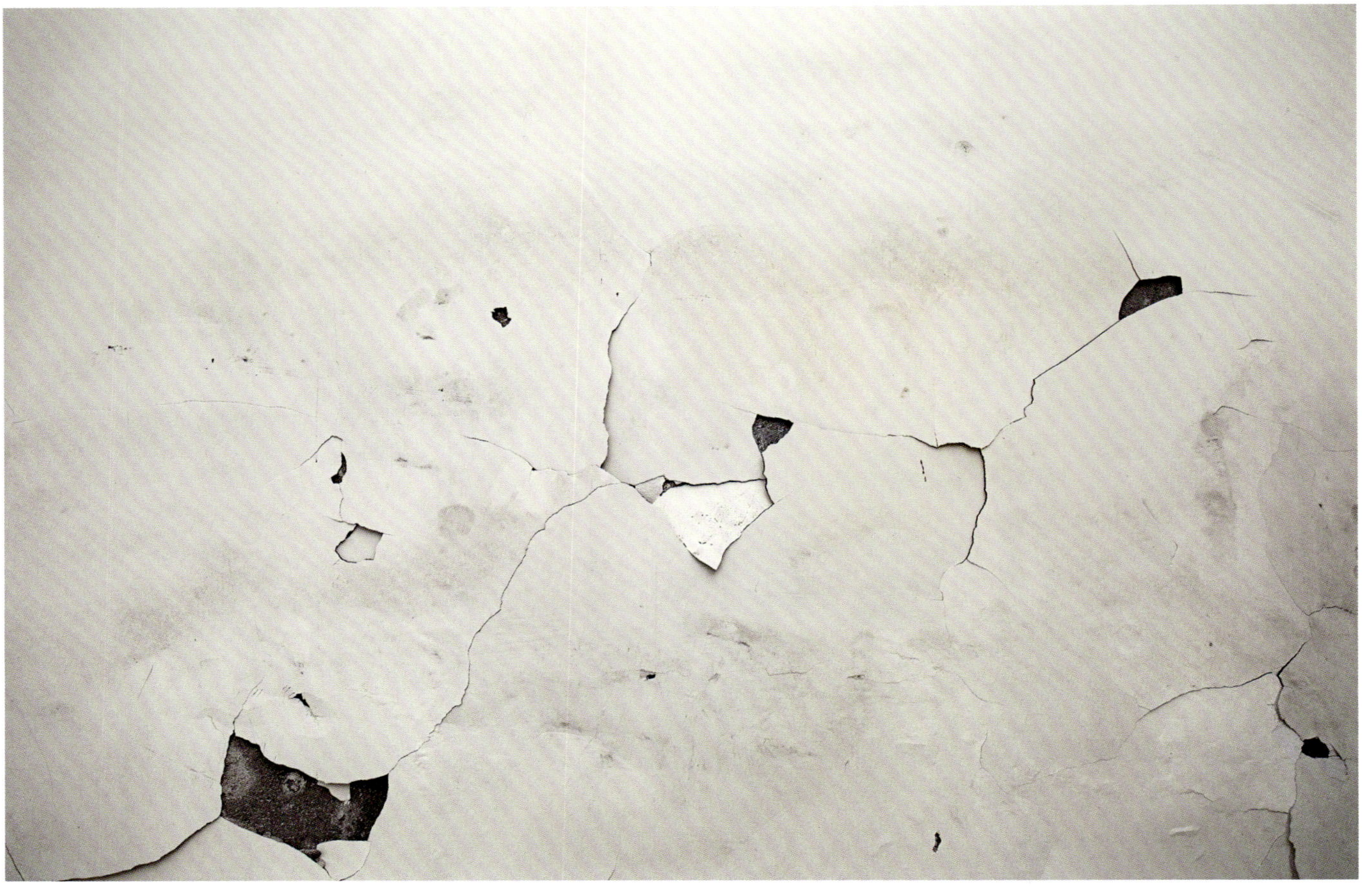

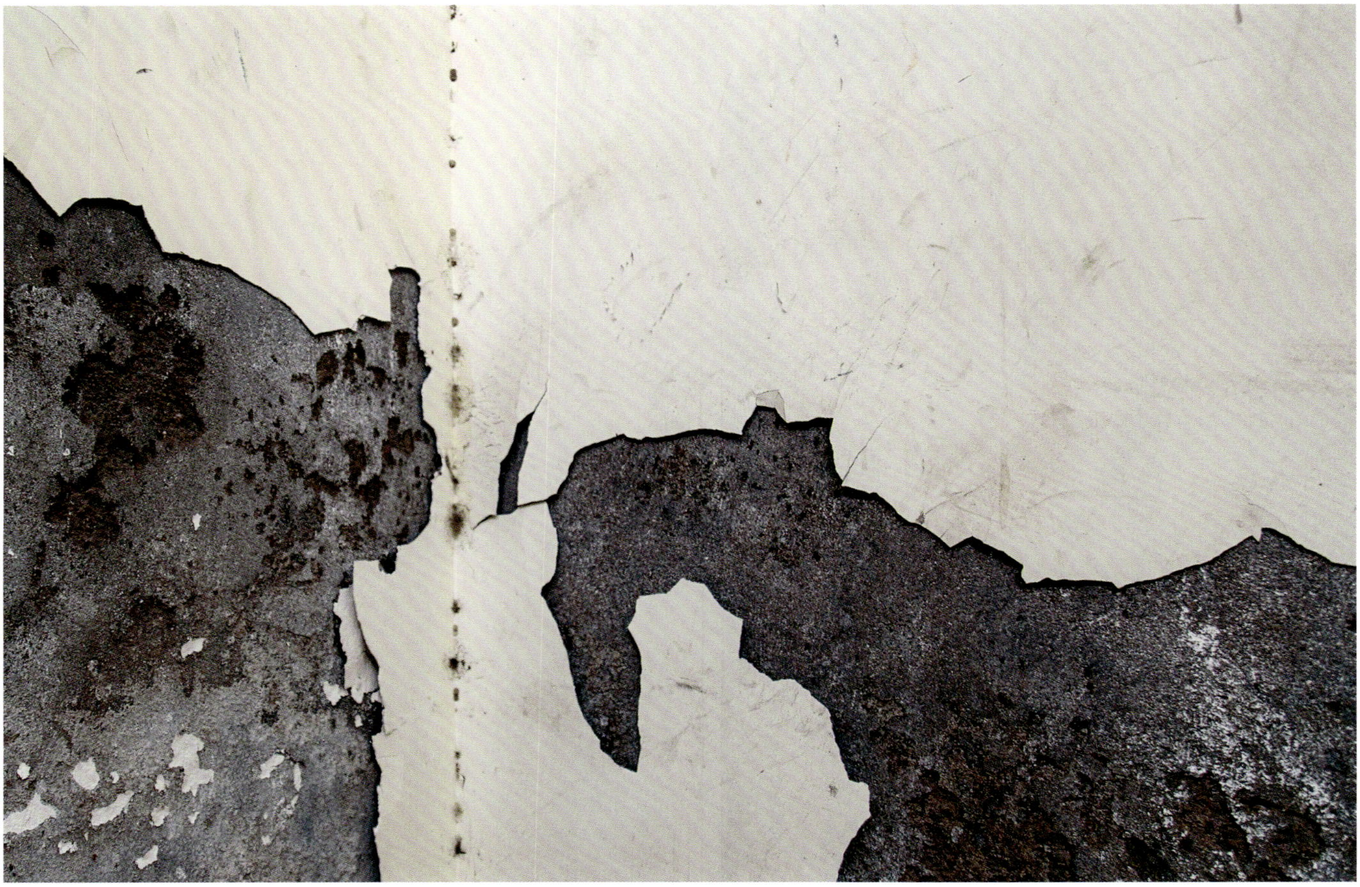

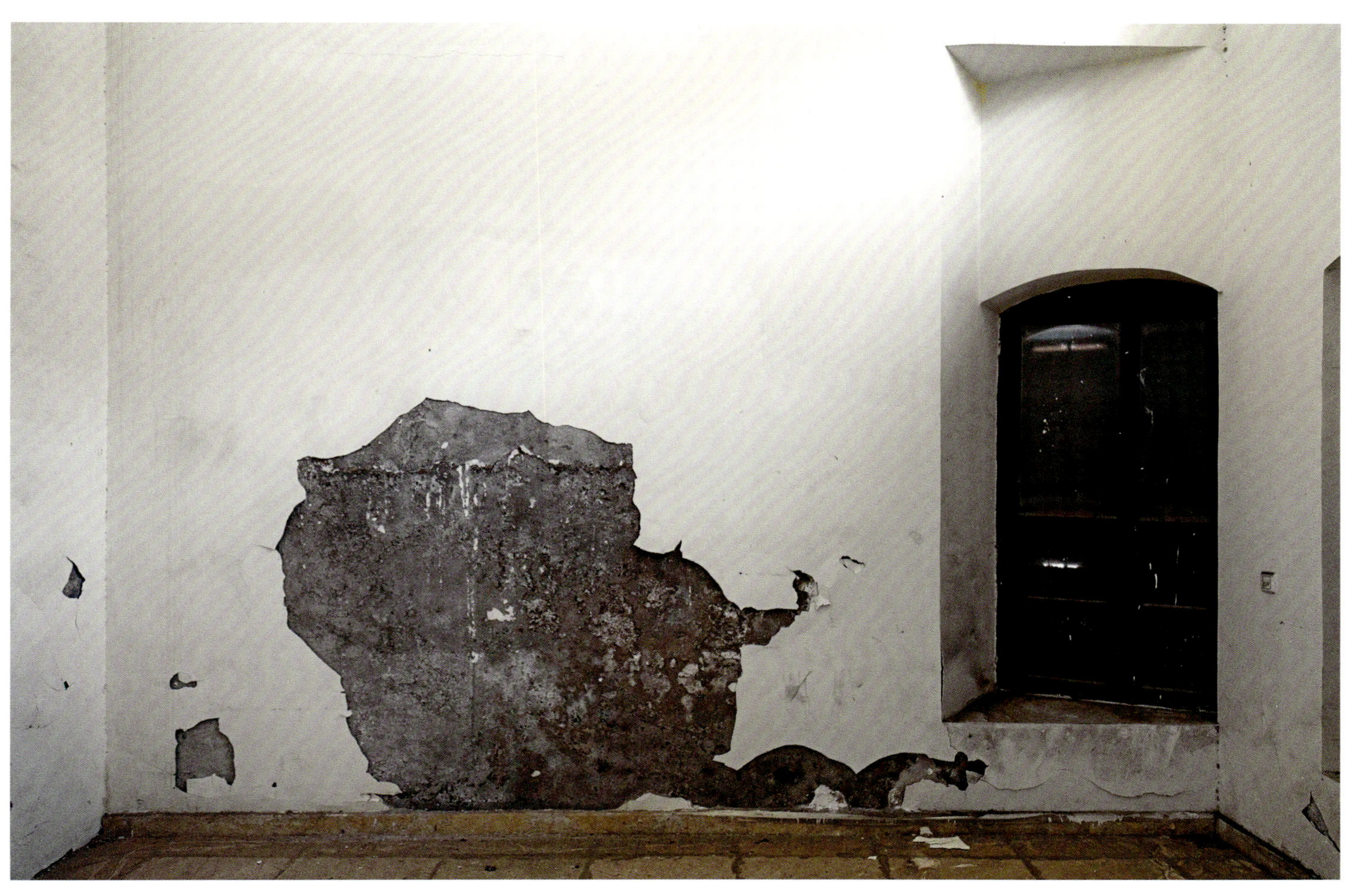

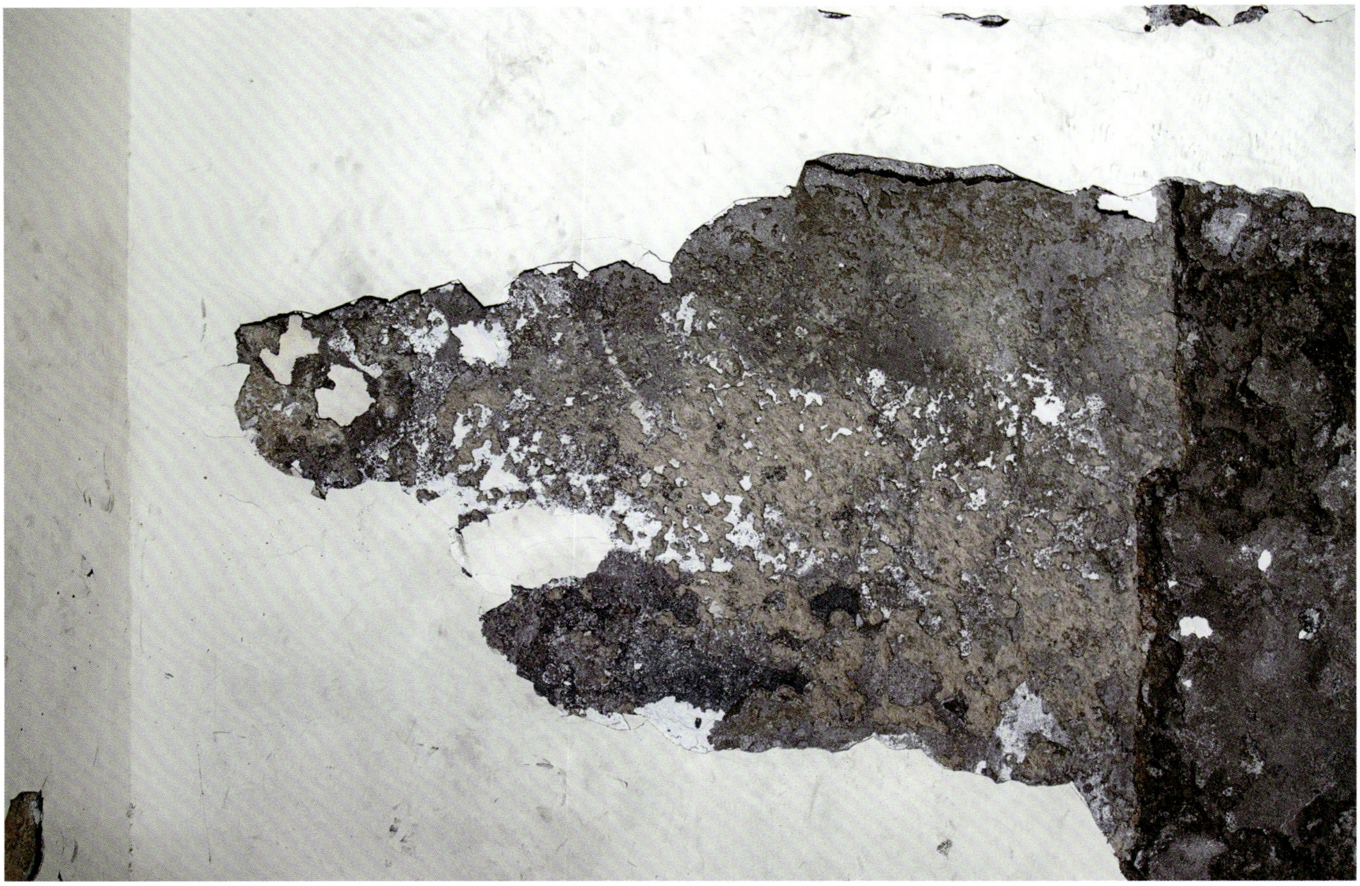

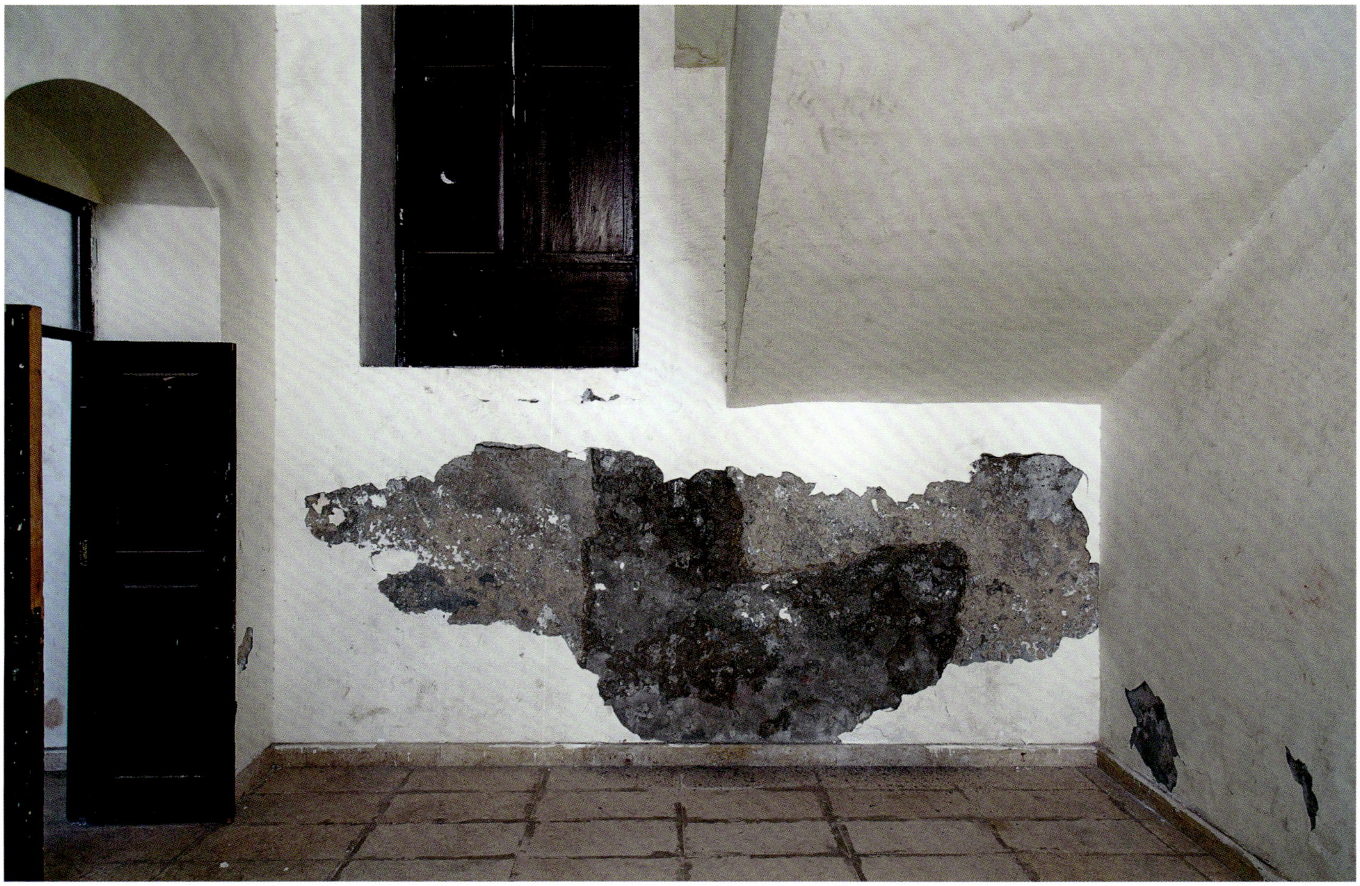

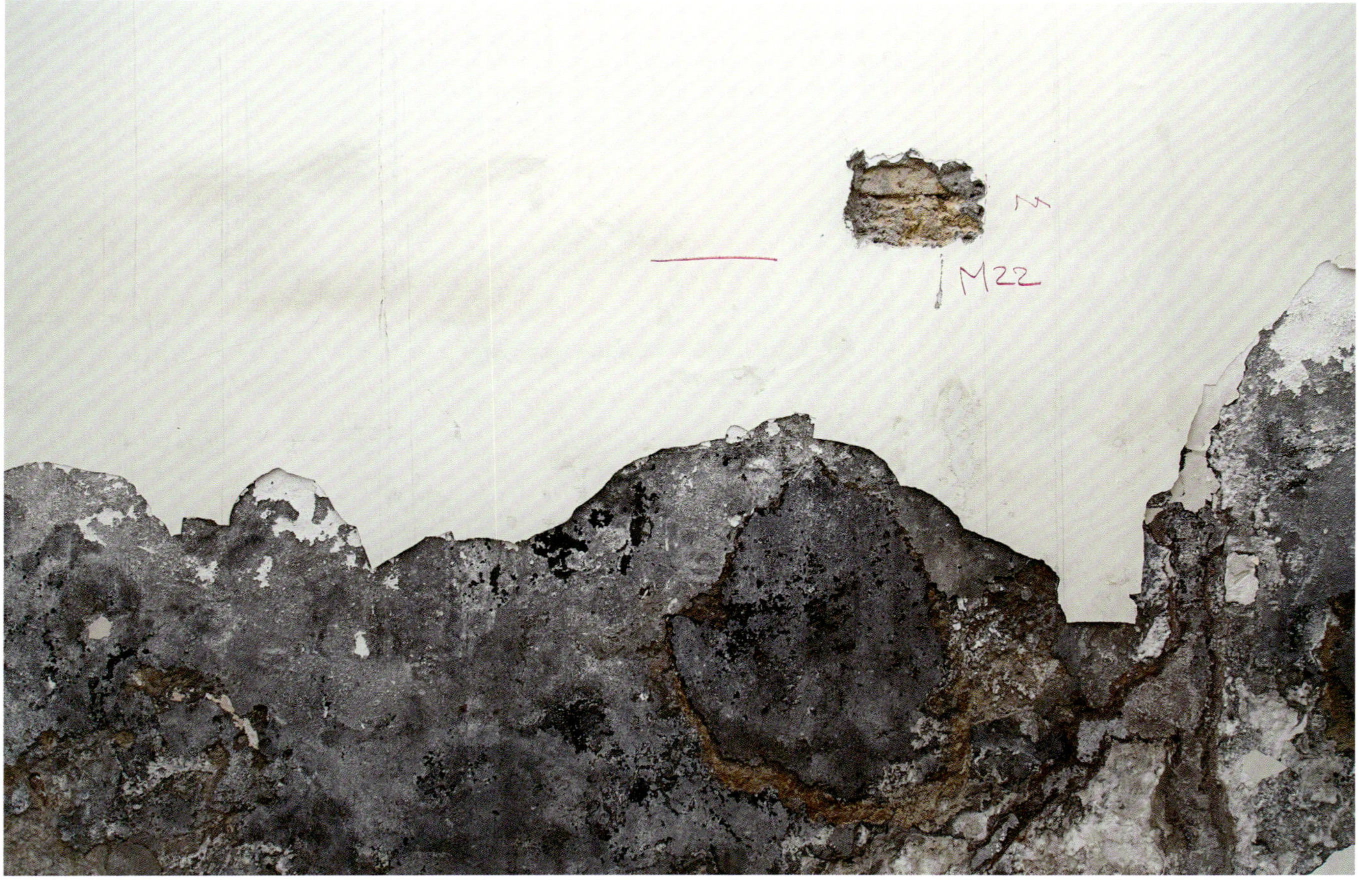

M22

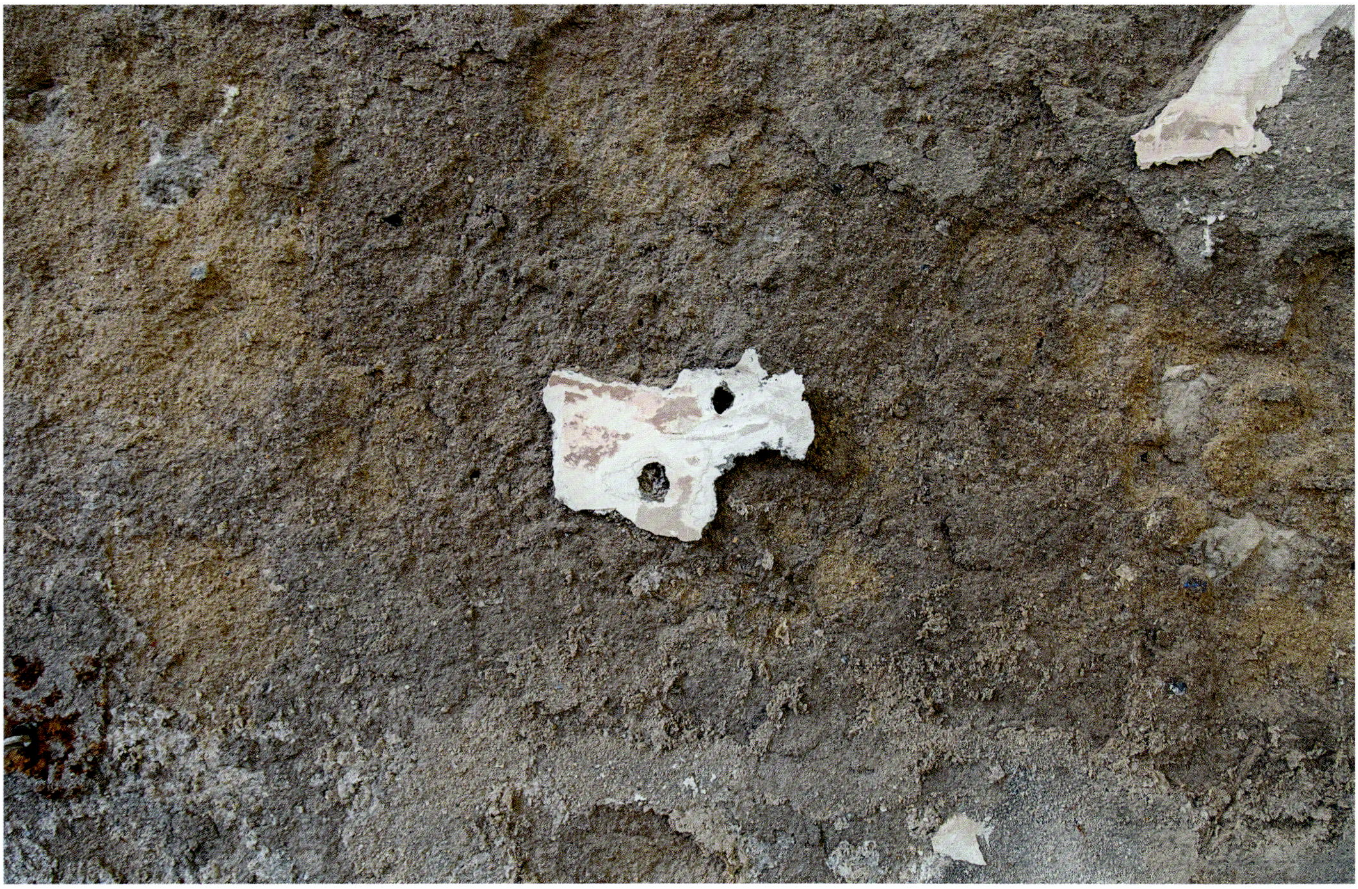

IV.

Paraphernalia

This emptiness is populated by many remainders, scattered and disparate elements that escaped the labor of the movers. These forgotten objects, stubbornly resisting removal, were to allow Moath Alofi to give his humor and virtuosity free rein; they too, in their own way, constitute signs, traces, and marks that the photographer would latch onto.

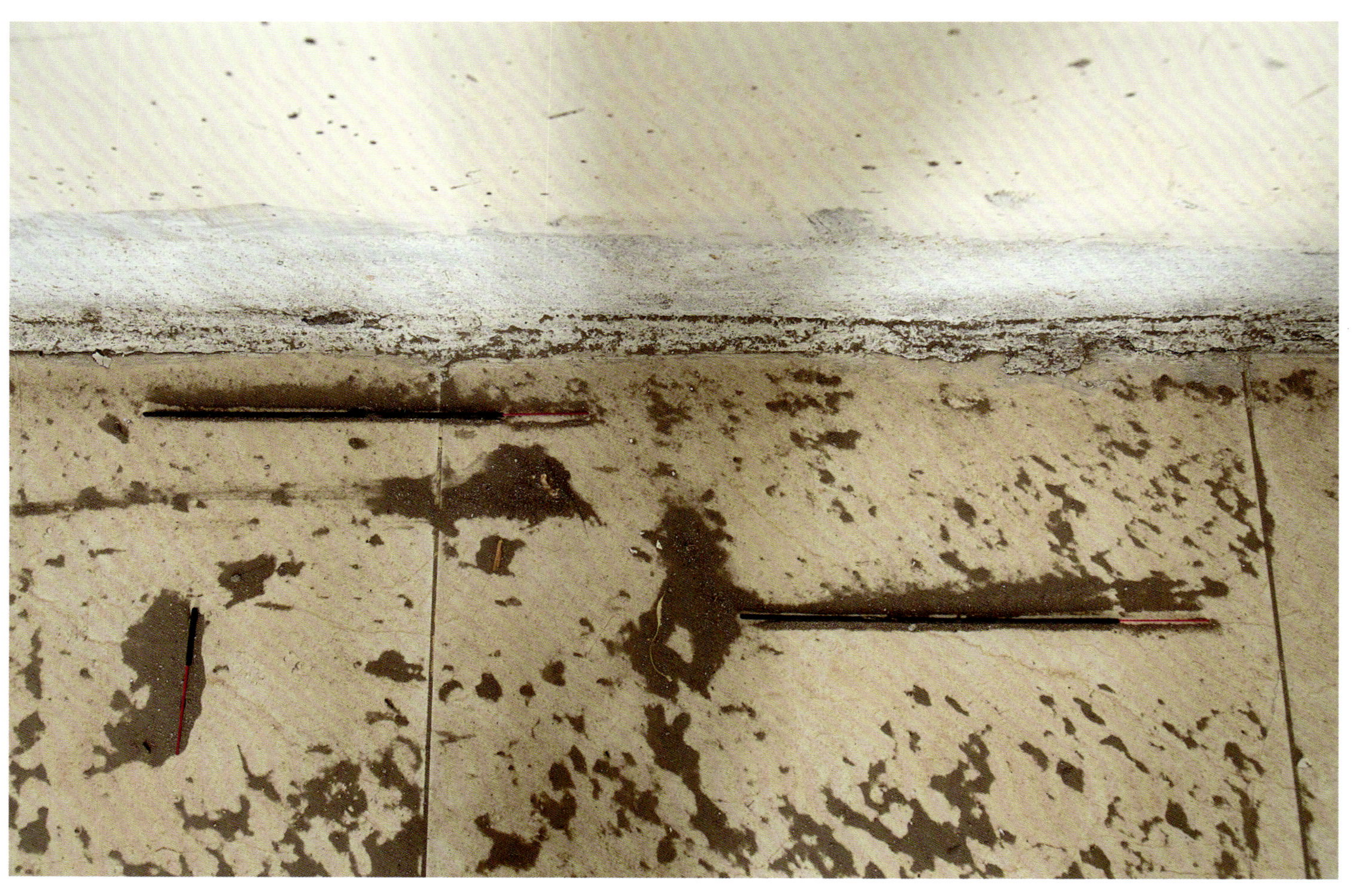

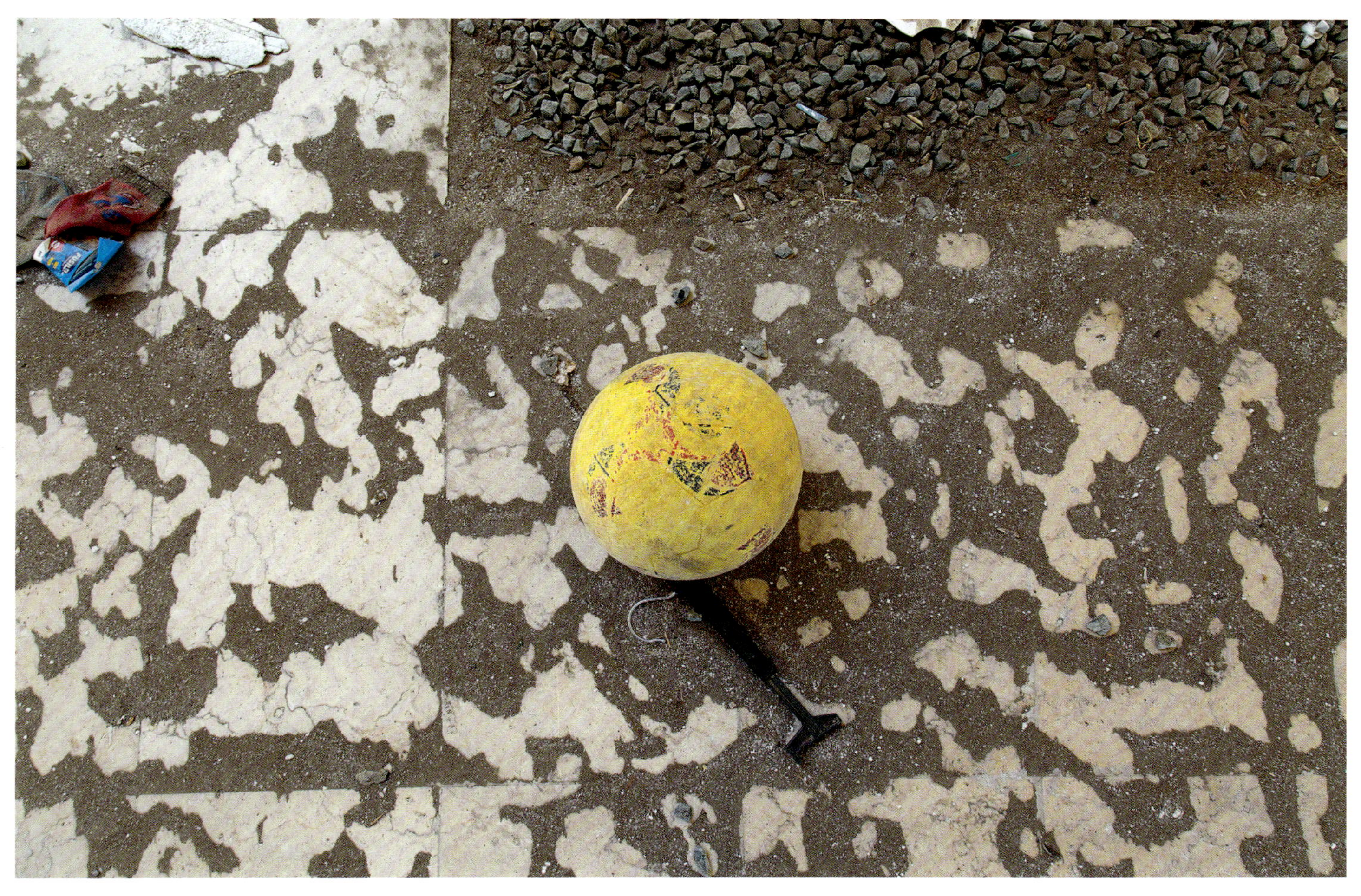

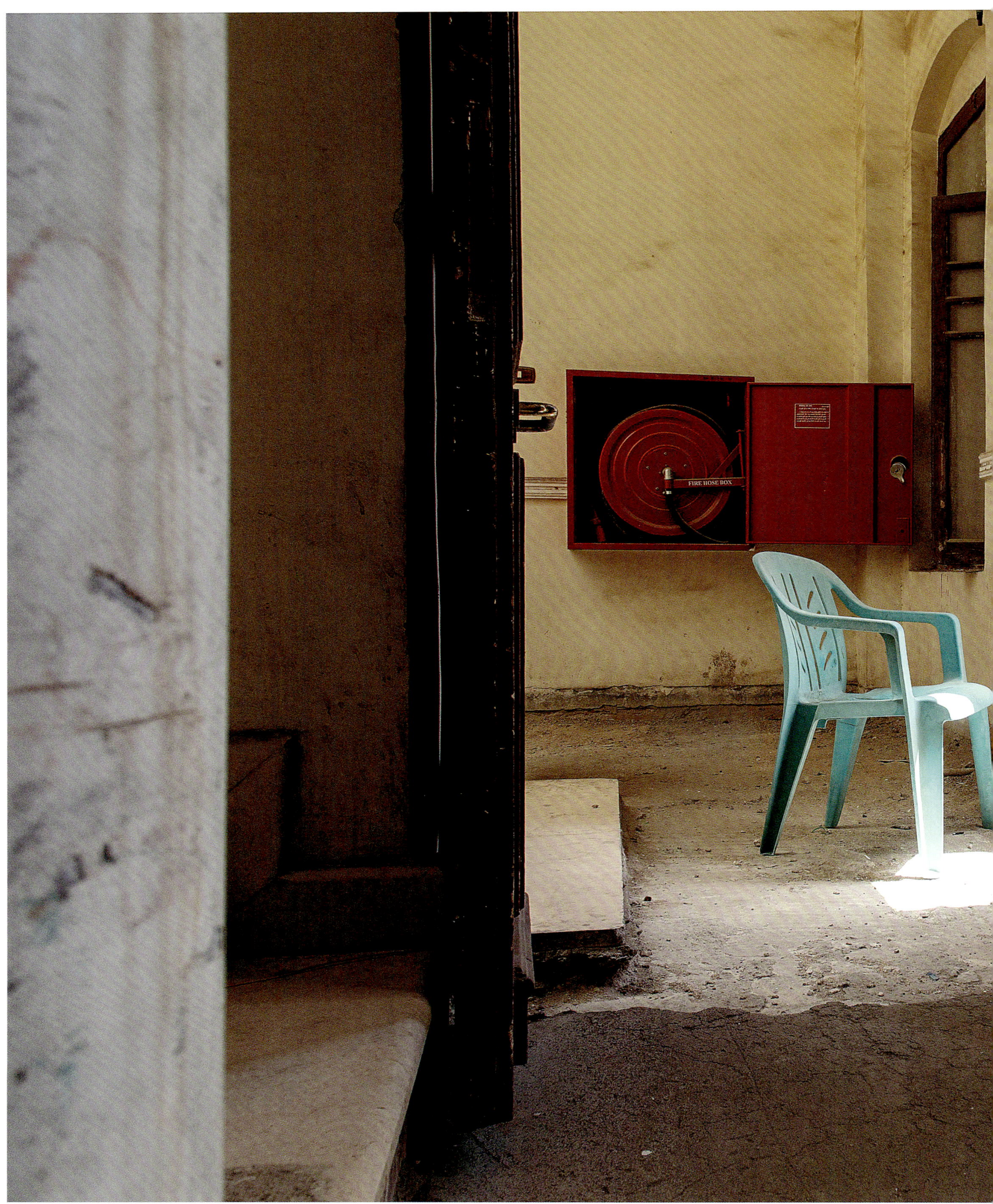
FIRE HOSE BOX

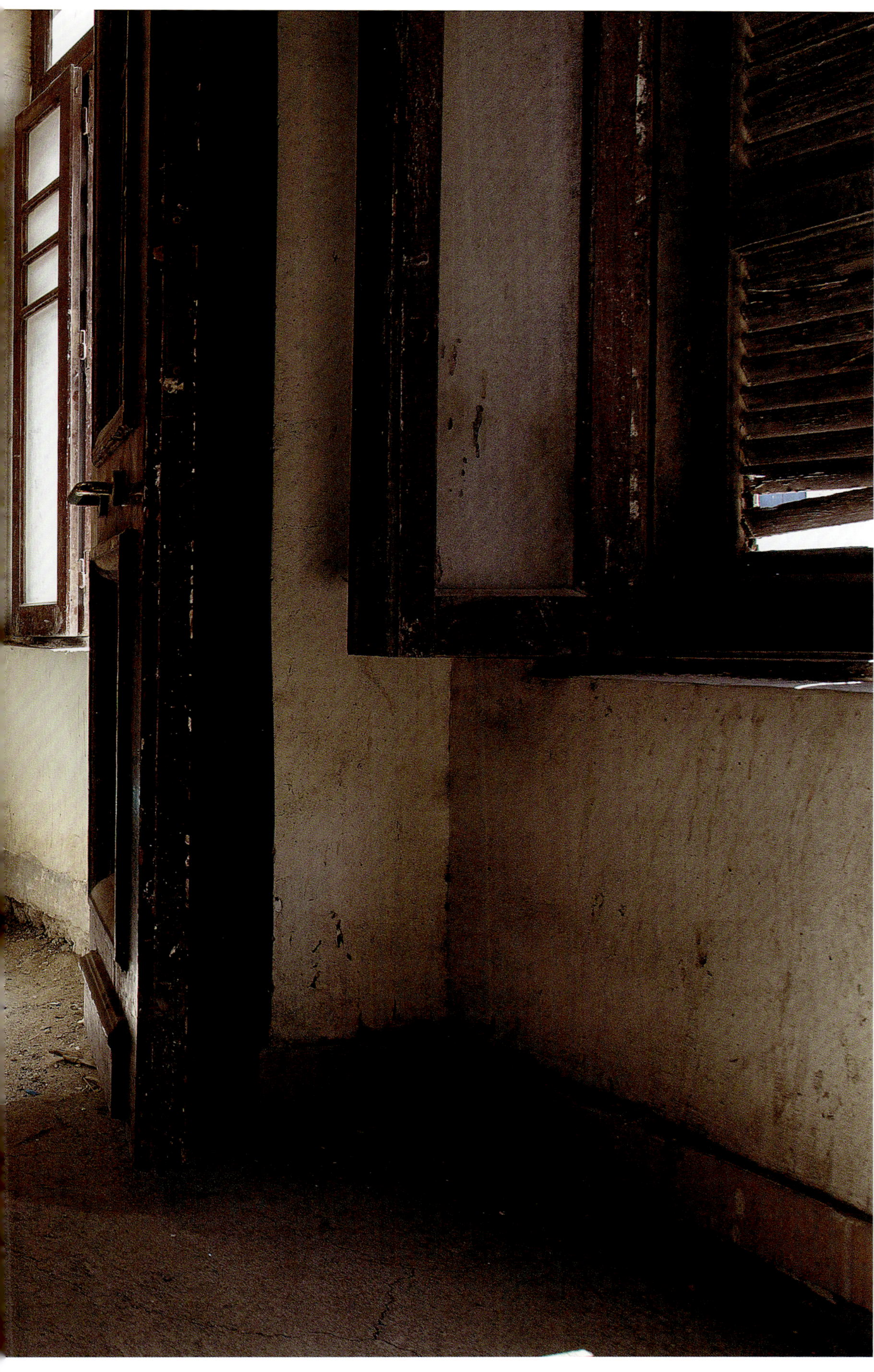

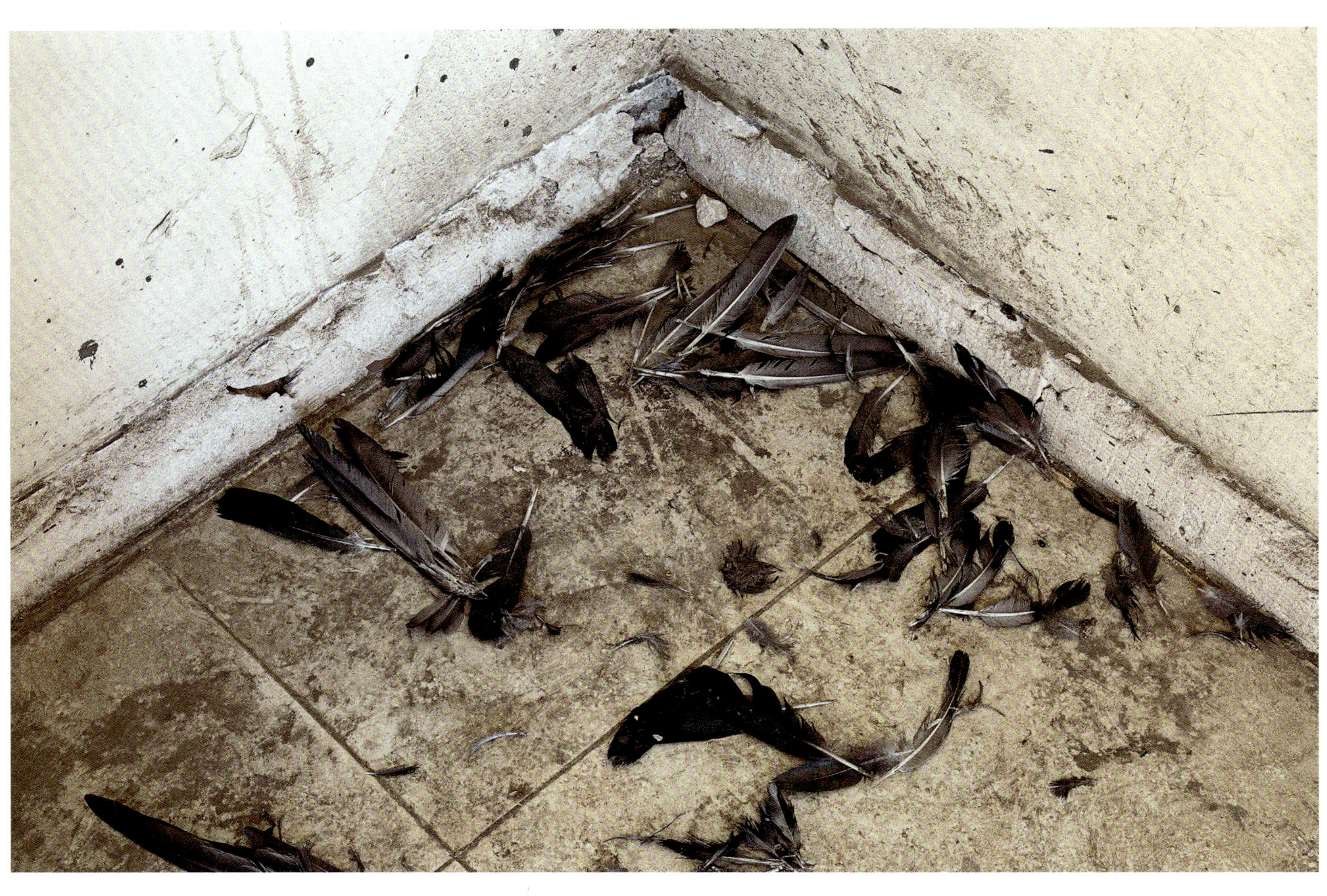

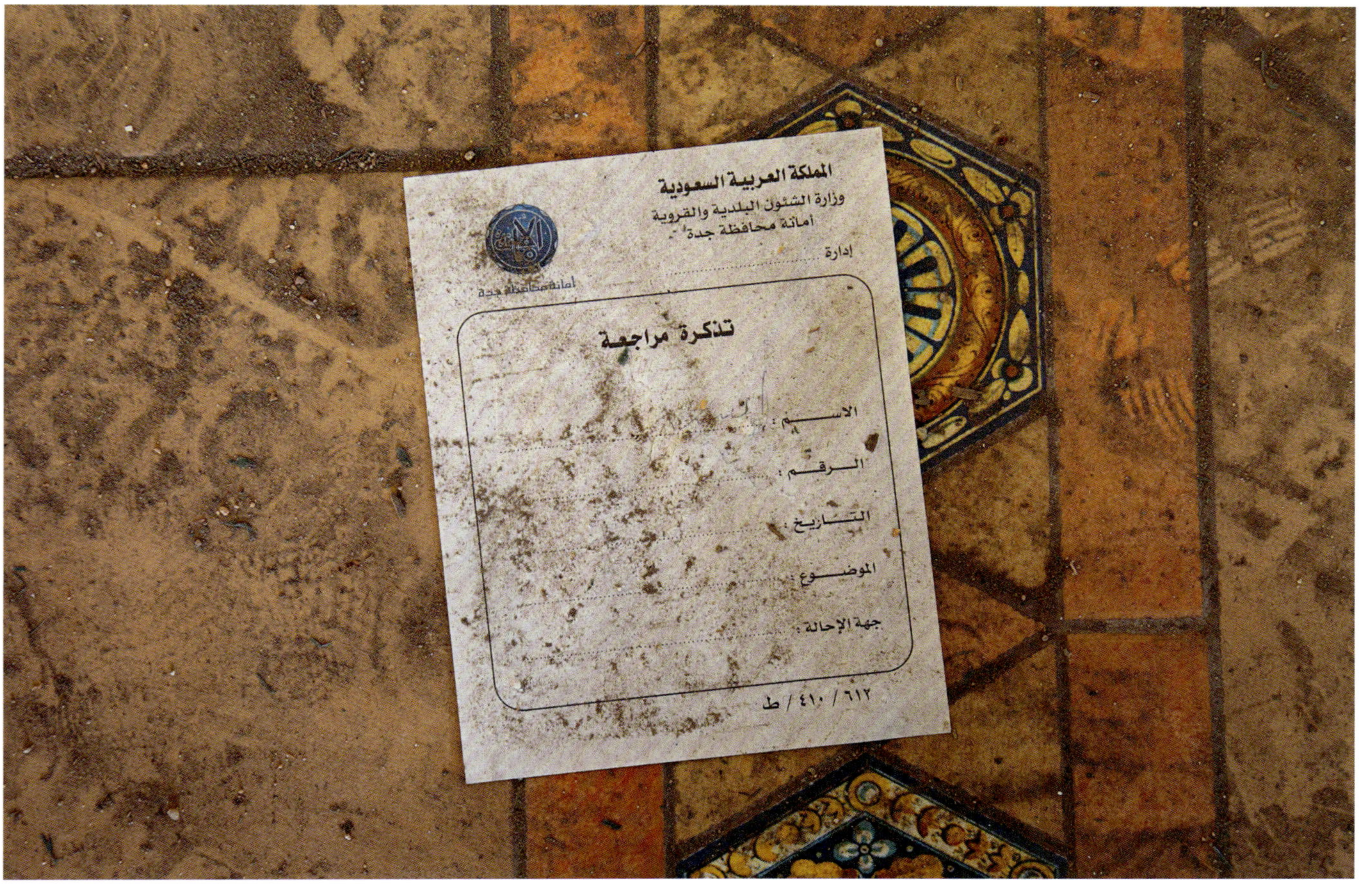

المملكة العربية السعودية
وزارة الشئون البلدية والقروية
أمانة محافظة جدة
أمانة محافظة جدة
إدارة
تذكرة مراجعة
الاســـم :
الــرقـــم :
التـــاريخ :
الموضـــوع :
جهة الإحالة :
٦١٢ / ٤١٠ / ط

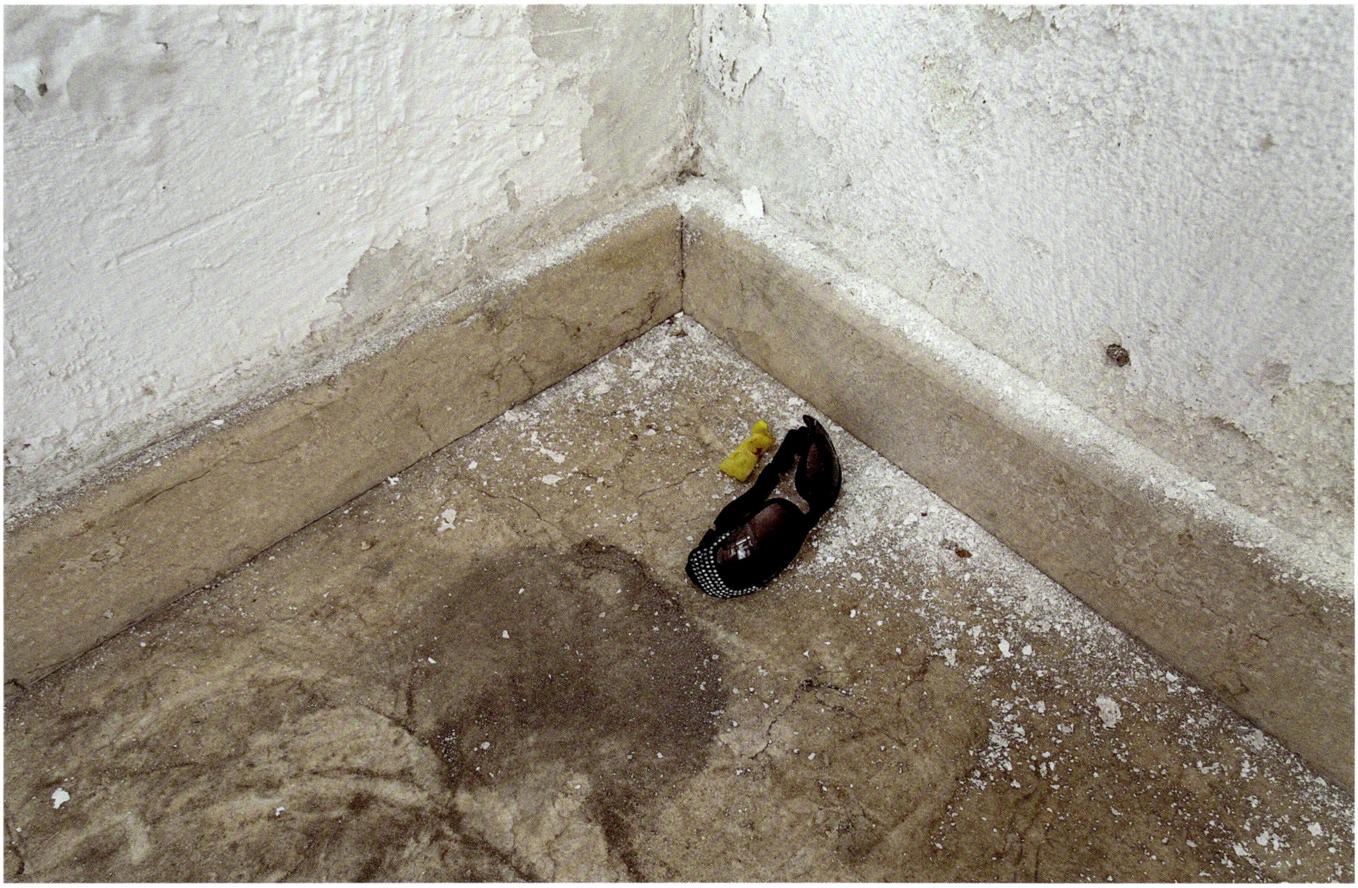

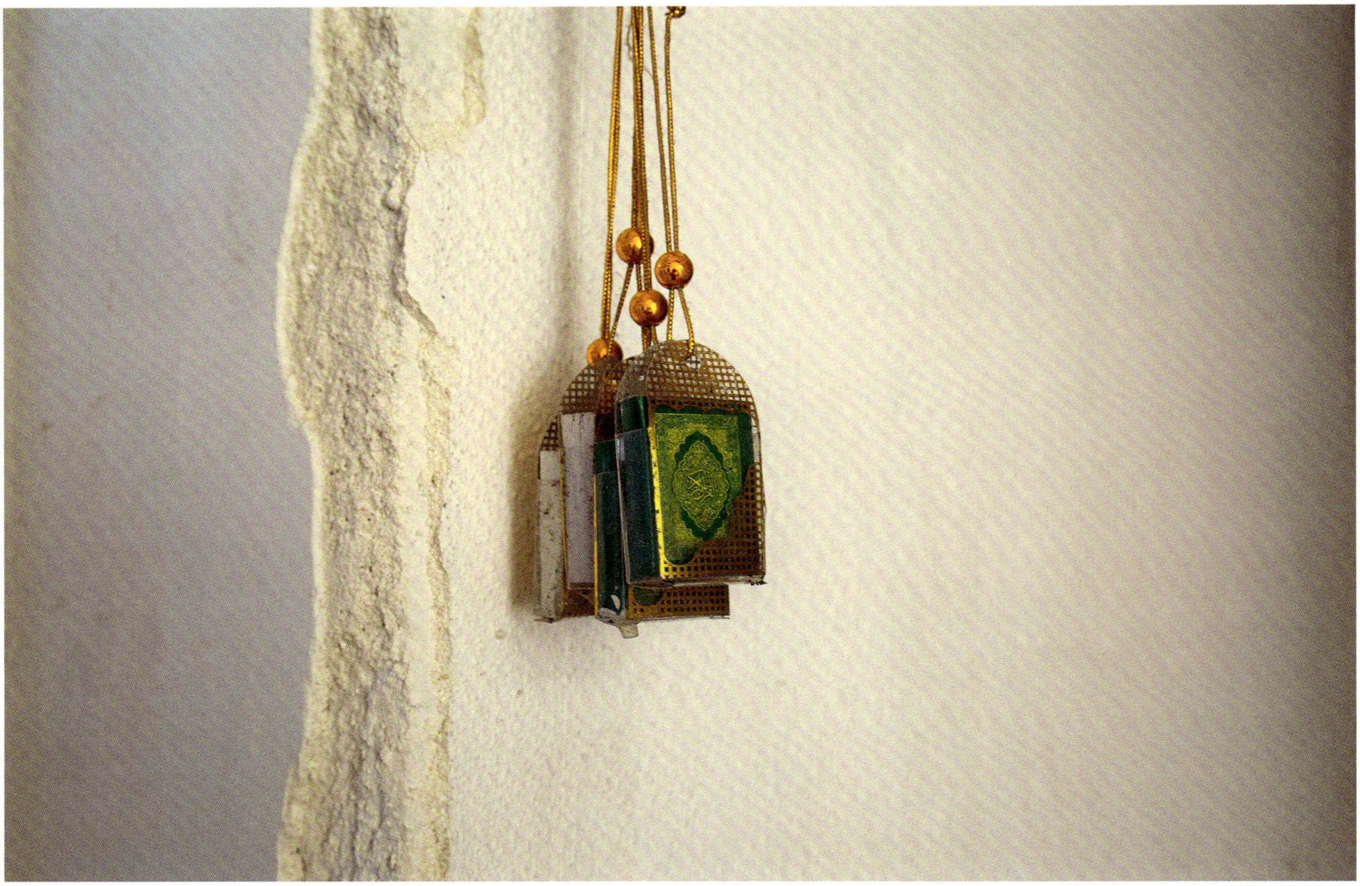

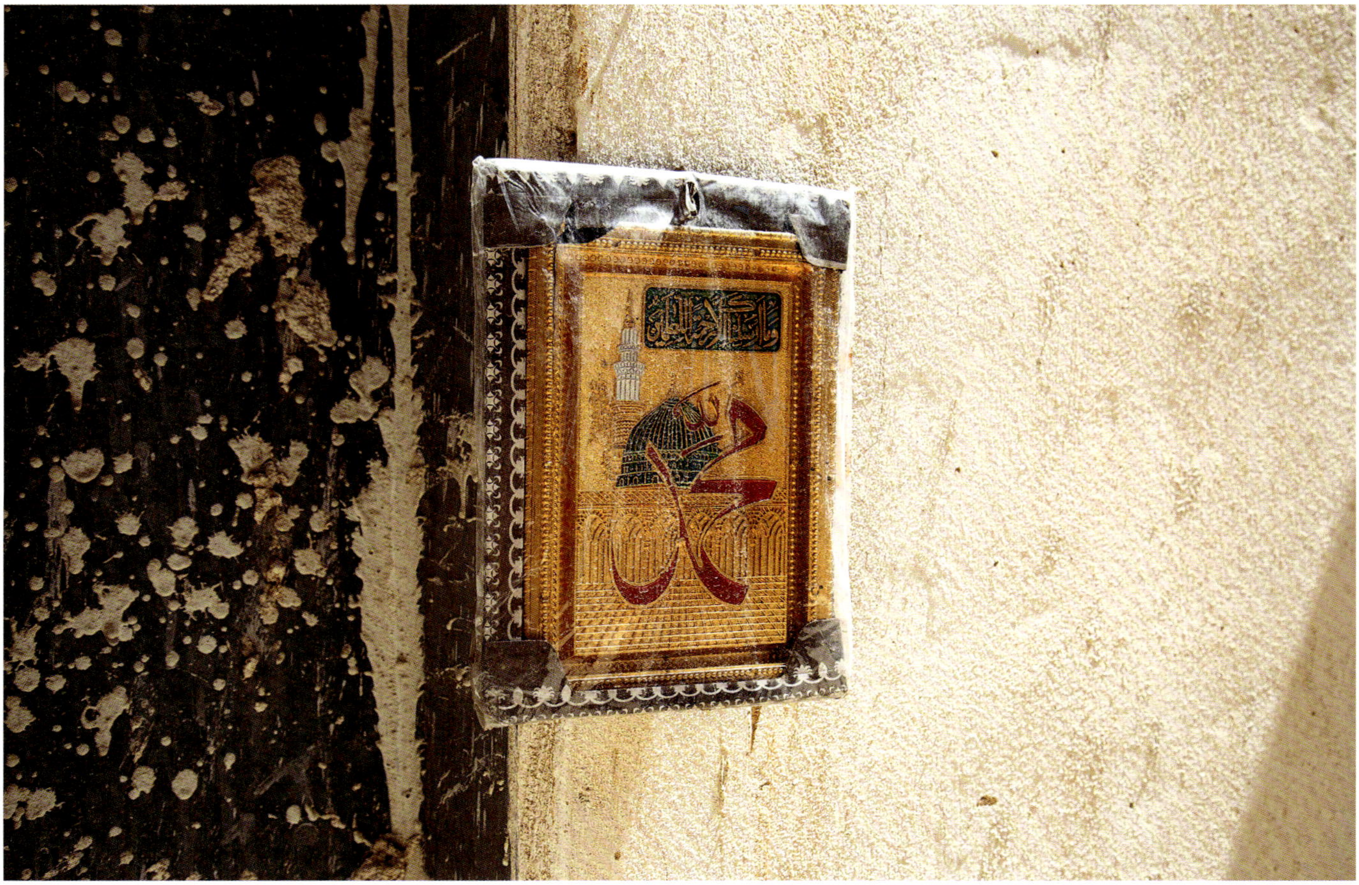

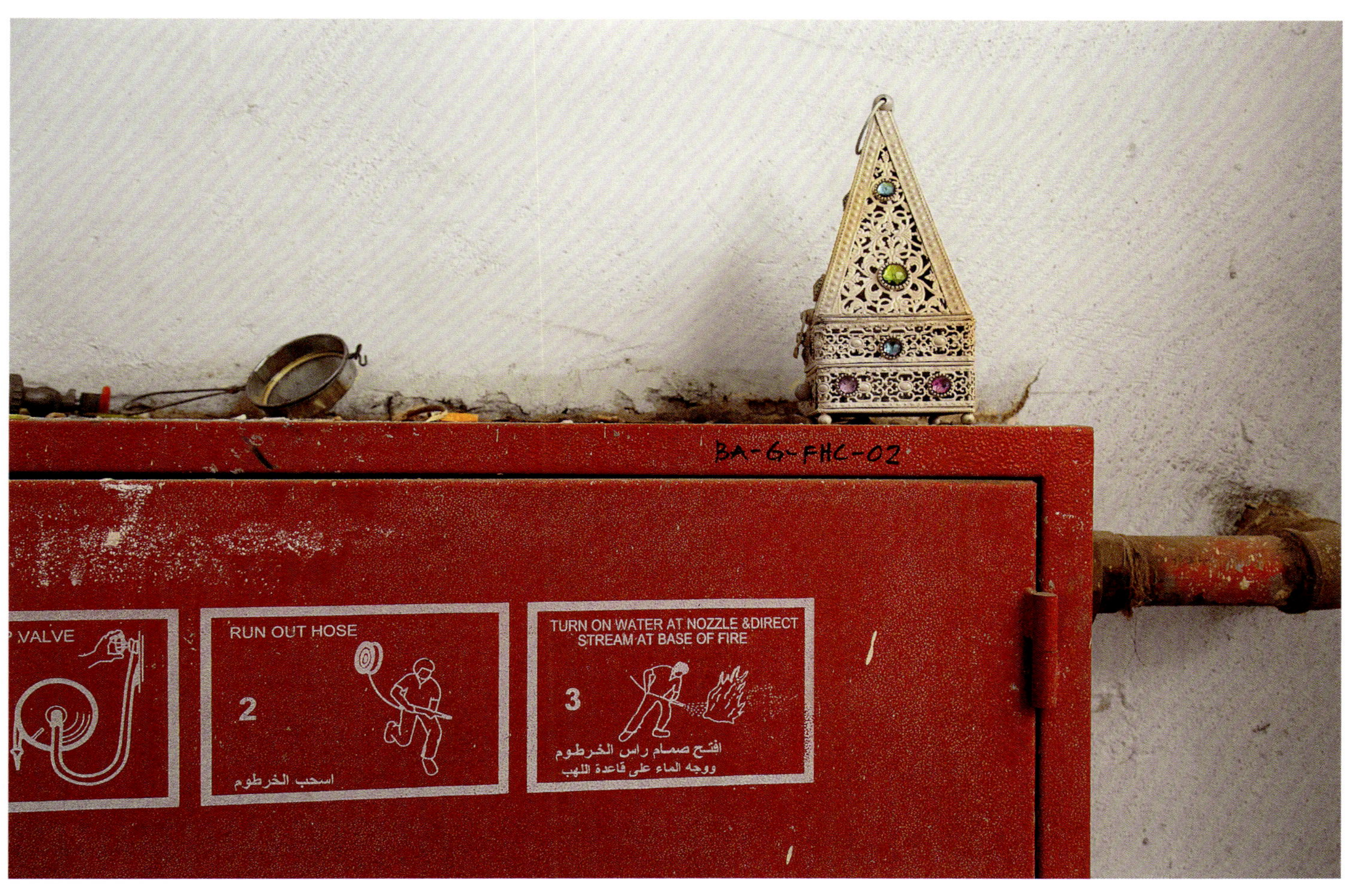

BA-6-FHC-02
VALVE
RUN OUT HOSE
2
اسحب الخرطوم
TURN ON WATER AT NOZZLE &DIRECT
STREAM AT BASE OF FIRE
3
افتح صمام راس الخرطوم
ووجه الماء على قاعدة اللهب

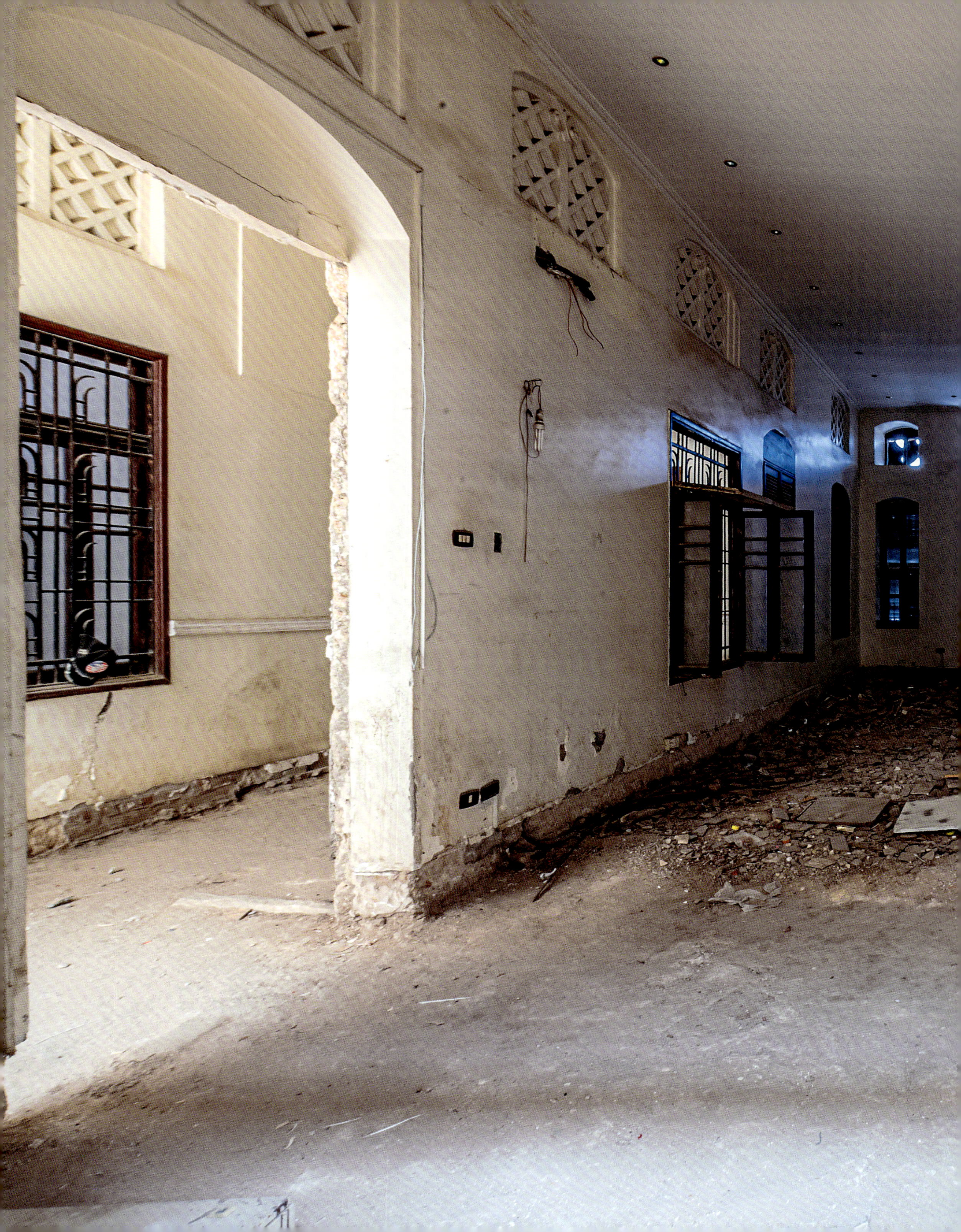

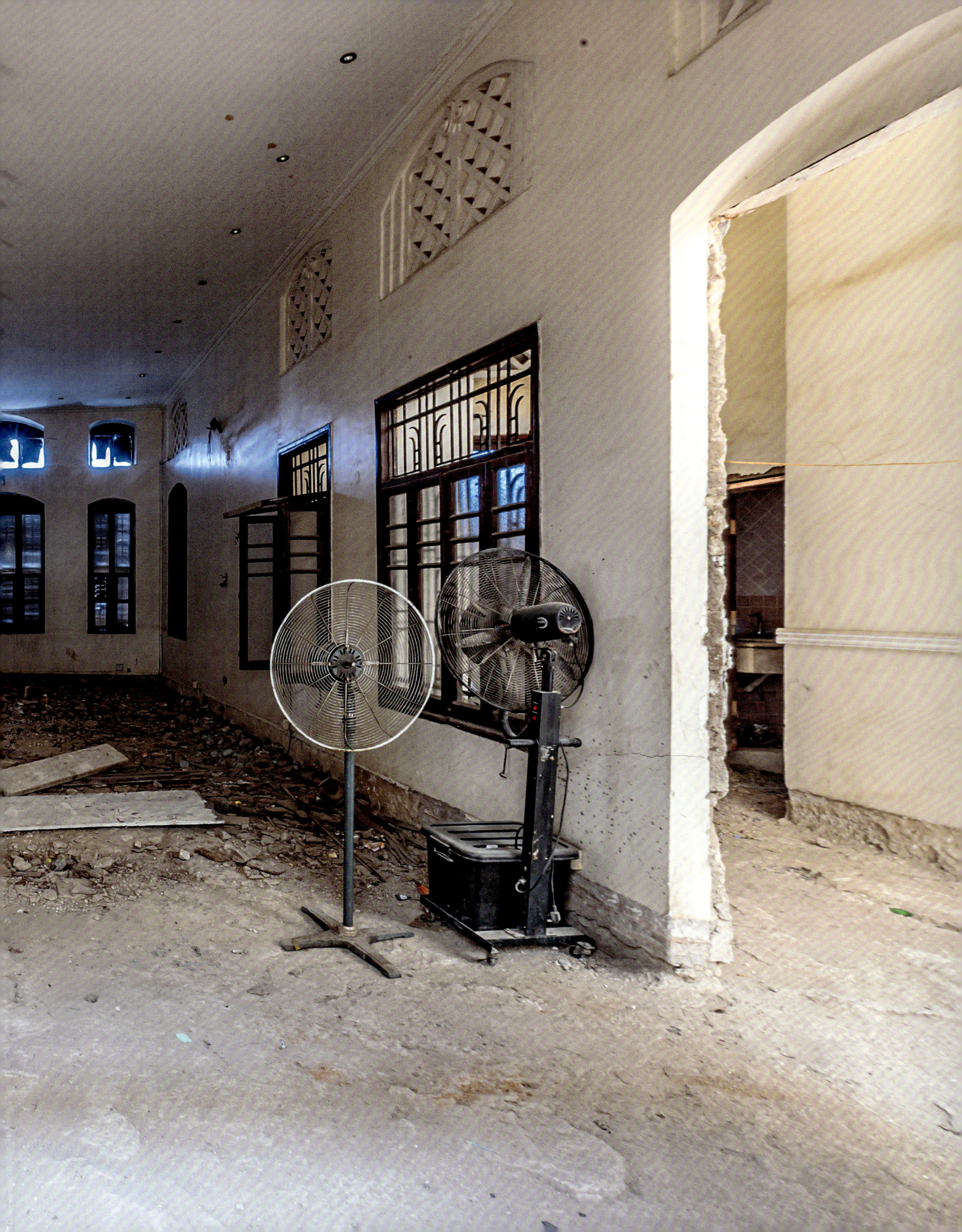

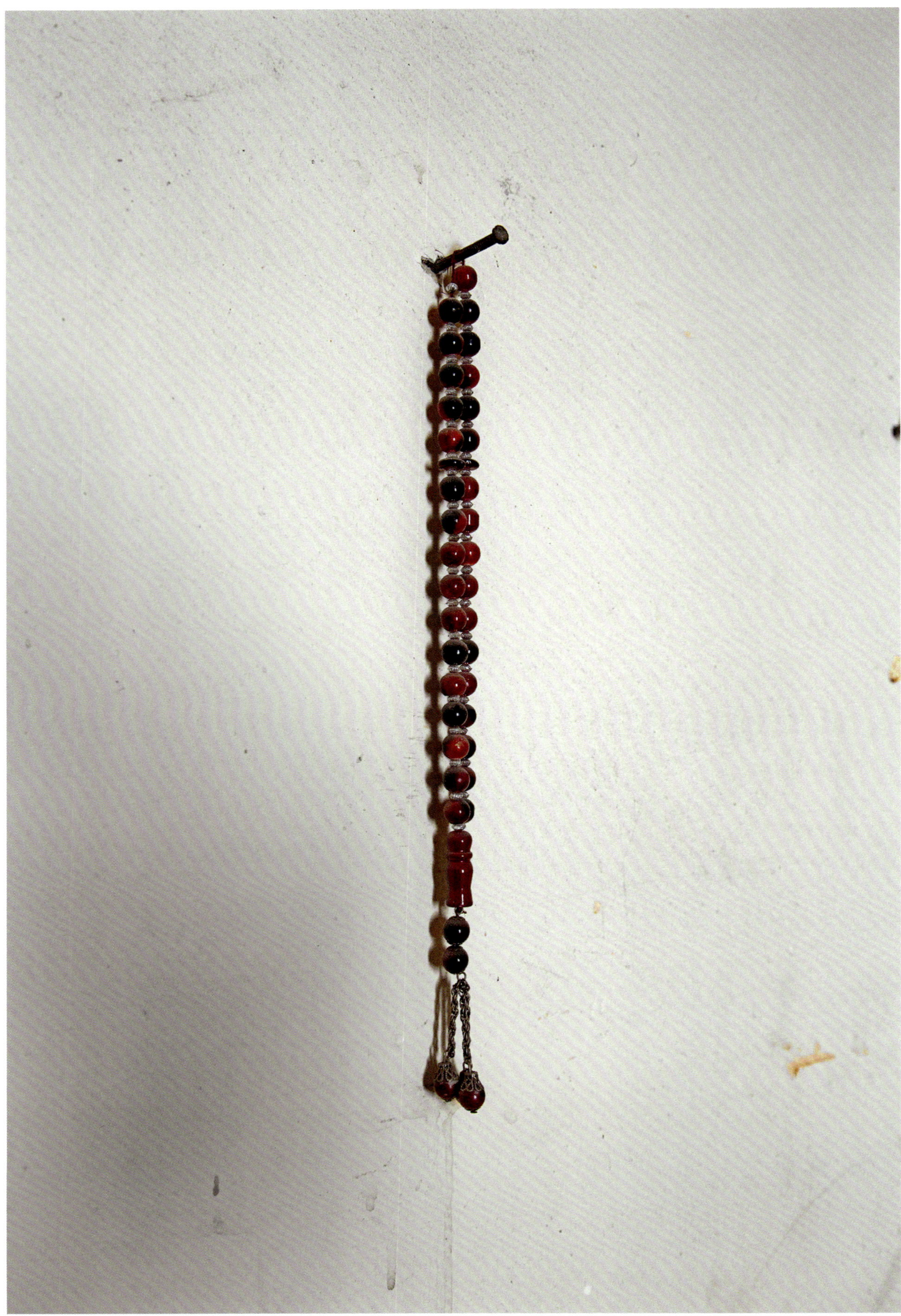

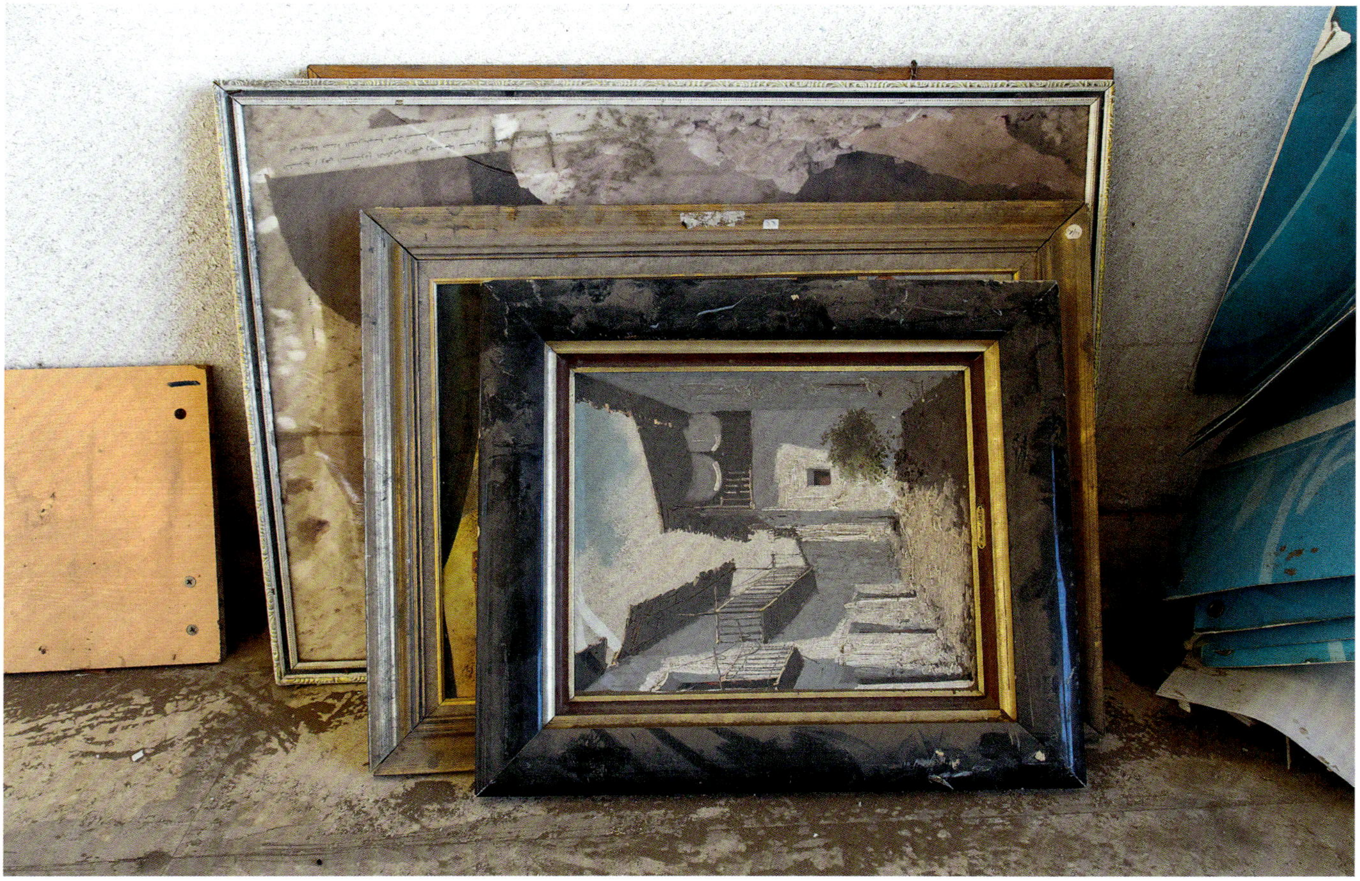

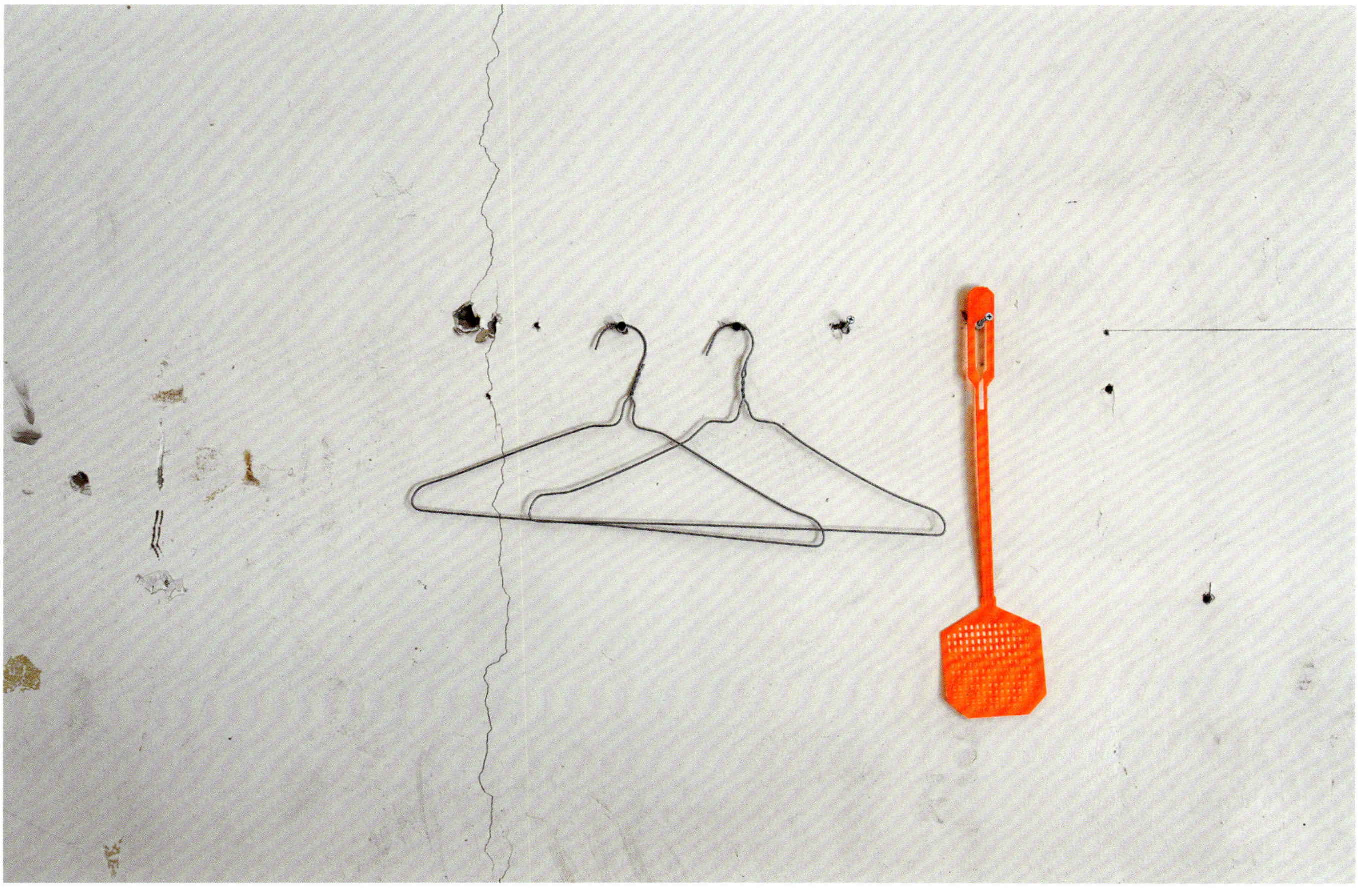

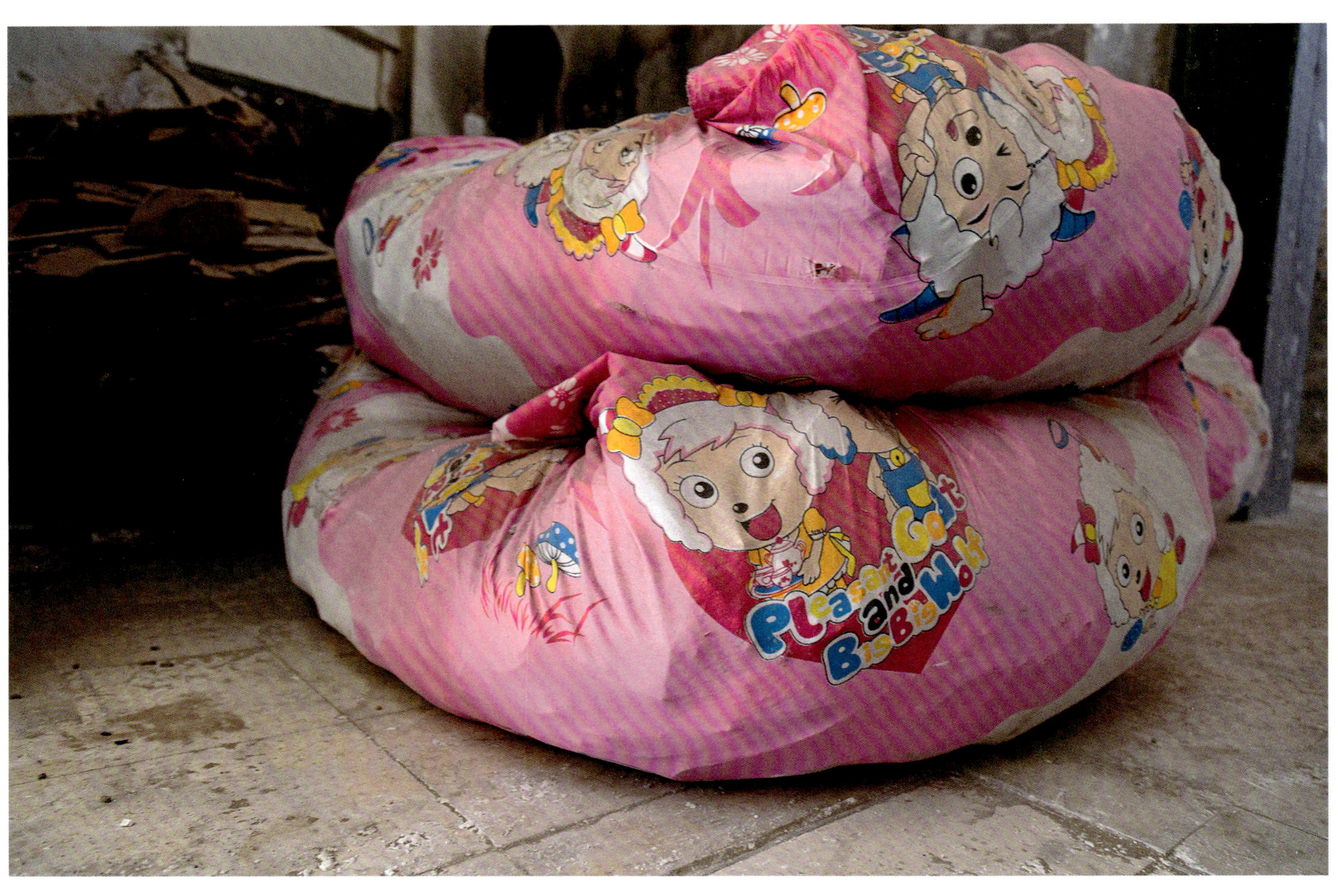

Pleasant Goat
and
Big Big Wolf

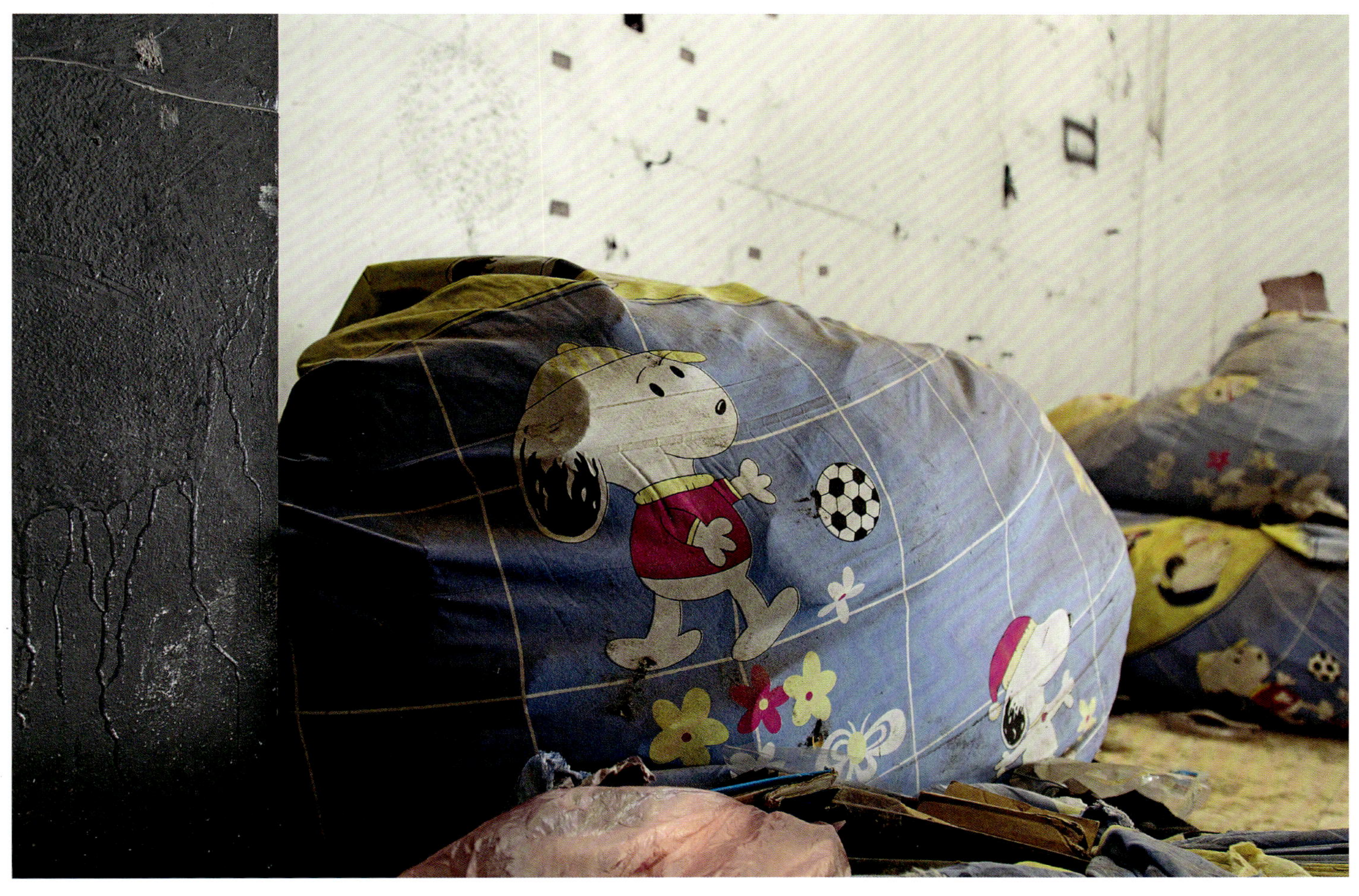

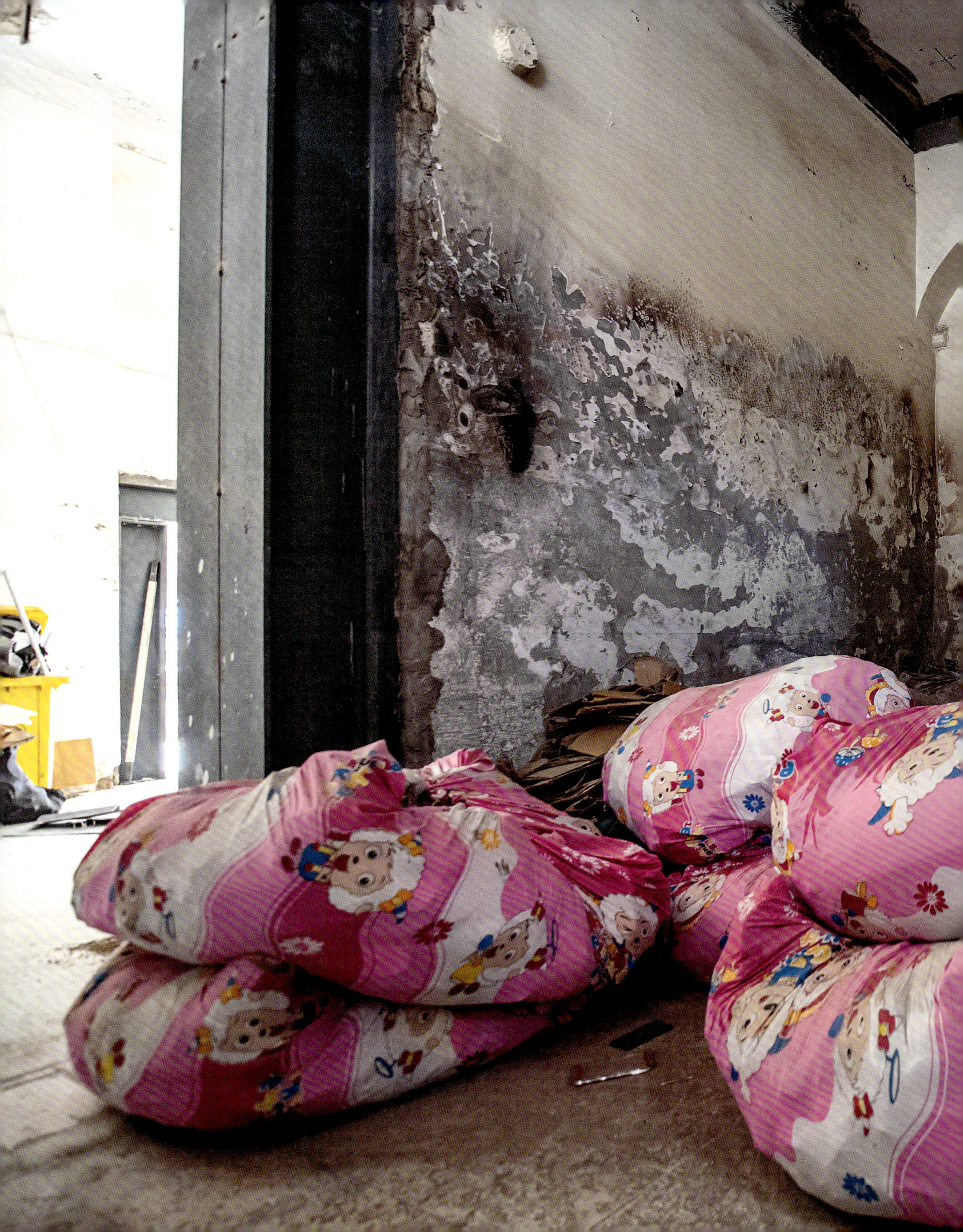

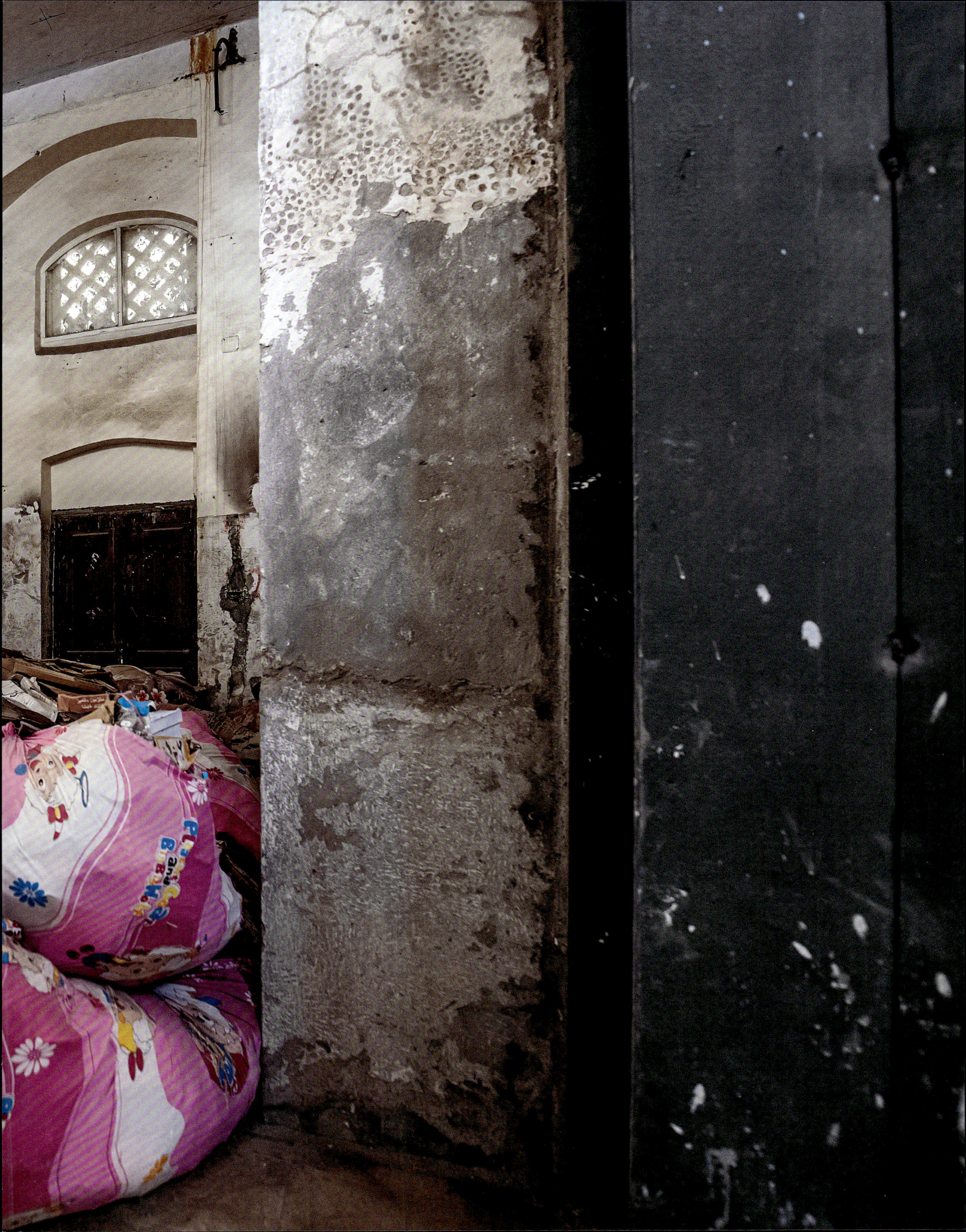

Moath Alofi

This son of Madinah has come a long way. Moath Alofi's works have been shown in France, Belgium, Switzerland, Russia, the United States, England, and South Korea. However, it was on the soil of Arabia that he accomplished his most far-reaching journeys. First of all, in Madinah. Then in the immediate surroundings of his hometown. Later, in the Hejaz region and across the whole territory of the kingdom. As art critic Mark Holborn very judiciously highlights in the introduction to Moath Alofi's beautiful book of photographs, recently published and entitled *Nabawi*.[1] "Madinah is the starting point of his creative work." Madinah is also and simultaneously "his home and his studio," as Moath Alofi himself describes it.[2]

"Moath Alofi could draw a map that charted the zones of his imagination," writes Mark Holborn, again, in *Nabawi*. The book is dedicated to the Great Mosque of Madinah and its followers. Known as the Prophet's Mosque, it harbors Muhammad's tomb, the Prophet and founder of Islam. Mark Holborn continues: "In the center of al-Masjid al-Nabawi [the Prophet's Mosque], is a chamber containing the tomb. From this spot the mosque and the city radiate outwards. Beyond the tomb is the mosque itself. Beyond the mosque and its continually expanding territory, the city stretches to remote districts in the foothills and up to the peaks or eastward across the lava fields towards the central deserts of the kingdom." Around the mausoleum that celebrates the Prophet even in death, it is life that abounds, crowds that swarm and the city that proliferates. The concentricity of the themes and subjects of interest that the photographer adapts seem to have come naturally to him from the outset.

A detail of his biography is particularly enlightening in this respect. Upon his return from Australia, with his degree in his pocket,[3] Moath Alofi experienced a real culture shock in Madinah, his home community.[4] It was to mitigate this shock that he felt the irrepressible need to turn to art and decided to embark on a career in photography, choosing from the outset to devote this creative energy to his native city and region. From the first, a dialectic of near and far founded his approach, which is oriented as much towards the present as it is to the past, sometimes even the most ancient of pasts.

His first works, *Walls of Medina* (2016), as well as *Doors of Barlik* (2017), show a city – his own – caught in the trap of frantic modernization and marked by the stigmata of this ineluctable expansion. *The Last Tashahhud* (2017) is dedicated to the particularly sparse prayer rooms – usually comprised of four simple walls and a door – dotted along the roads around Madinah, serving as wayside shelters for travelers and offered to them by the generosity of a few philanthropists. The prosaic character of the architectural elements is striking and central to these three series of images. The simplicity of the subjects chosen, as well as the sobriety with which Moath Alofi treats them, did not however form an obstacle to the inchoate development of a highly personal aesthetic, which is deployed as closely as possible to reality.

Moath Alofi also often turns to the past, for instance in a remarkable series of photographs entitled *People of Pangaea* (2018). In some sense, it is to the other end of History that the photographer leads those who, thanks to him, discover images of these extraordinary stone structures, several hundreds of which punctuate the desert foothills of the region of Madinah. The oldest of these were built some nine thousand years ago. They had been rediscovered, early last century, by the first pilots to fly over this region of the world, since they are much more visible and detectable from the sky. It is in this way that Moath Alofi presents them to us. These constructions are the work of the desert civilizations of the Neolithic period, about which we know very little. Neither historians nor ethnologists have managed to solve their mystery. Their walls sometimes stretch across several hundreds of meters, and their plans adopt widely diverse forms. They required the participation of a great many individuals to build them.

What was their purpose? Were they – as was long thought and some continue to believe – highly sophisticated gazelle traps? Or, more simply, cattle folds? Or, funerary enclosures? Places of worship? Moath Alofi does not take sides. His intentions are very different: "I want to shock you, I want to make you wonder, ask questions; get you to search and arouse curiosity in the audience," he explains regarding some of the images he presents.[5] It is not so much landscapes that Moath Alofi shows as it is the efforts – sometimes considerable – undertaken by individuals to inscribe their mark within it. So, in a vertiginous reversal, we might say that despite passing from one extremity of History to the other, Moath Alofi finds himself dealing with precisely the same subject, whether it be the highly contemporary prayer rooms of *The Last Tashahhud* or the enigmatic constructions in *People of Pangaea*. Both are dispersed throughout the landscapes of the region of Madinah, and the images that Moath Alofi gives us of them offer a unique window onto the human desire to merge into the territory and confront their fate.

This significance of humanity lies at the heart of Moath Alofi's work. "The presence or absence of people within a space is as fundamental as its architecture and topography," he notes in *Nabawi*, mentioned above.[6] The book bears the subtitle *Devotion in Madinah*. It expresses the prominent importance accorded to the faithful and visitors to the Great Mosque of Madinah, one of the most heavily visited places in the world. Alongside visitors from across the globe, the book presents the faces of shepherds from the surrounding area of Madinah, who were the subject of one of Moath Alofi's finest series of photographs, soberly entitled *Shepherds of Arabia* (2017). Concerning these portraits, art critic Mark Holborn wrote, most fittingly: "The weathering of their features, their folds and furrows has merged them with their geography. They 'become' the place they inhabit"[7] It is this constant to and fro – these correspondences between, on the one hand, the people and, on the other, the settings, sites, and territories that they inhabit – that forms the specificity and power of Moath Alofi's work. The coherence that emanates from Moath Alofi's various works evidently derives from the "unit of place" underpinning his entire corpus. Their homogeneity is due to the fact that he was able to foster and then develop within his work an aesthetic respectful of the particularities of his native region. In general terms, firmly established local roots and deliberate regionalism can paradoxically enable artworks to attain universality. It may well be that this holds true in the case of Moath Alofi's photographs.

Works

· *Walls of Medina*, 2016, photographic series
· *Doors of Barlik*, 2017, photographic series
· *Shepherds of Arabia*, 2017, photographic series
· *The Last Tashahhud*, 2017, photographic series
· *People of Pangaea*, 2018, photographic series
· *Mihlaiel*, 2018, video
· *Thad*, 2019, photographic and video archive
· *Naphtha*, Khuzam Palace, 2019, collective exhibition
· *Cyprium*, 2020, photographic series and installation
· *Nabawi. Devotion in Madinah*, 2021, photographic book

[1] Moath Alofi (photographer) and Mark Holborn (editor), *Nabawi. Devotion in Madinah* (Saudi Arabia: Thad for Arts, 2021), p. 21.
[2] Moath Alofi's personal website, www.moathalofi.com.
[3] Moath Alofi obtained his BA in Environmental Management and Sustainable Development from Bond University in Gold Coast, Australia, in 2013.
[4] Cf. article in *Esquire Middle East*, September 10, 2021.
[5] Interview with Moath Alofi by Mariam Nihal, *Saudi Gazette*, February 9, 2018.
[6] *Nabawi, op. cit*, p. 267.
[7] *Nabawi, op. cit*, p. 26.

The publication accompanies
the exhibition *The Gate of Gates*,
presented at the Red Sea Museum
in 2025.

Published by the Museums
Commission, Ministry of Culture,
Saudi Arabia and Skira editore.

Project Manager
Edoardo Ghizzoni

Project coordination
Hagar Adam, Ministry of Culture,
Saudi Arabia
Emma Cavazzini, Claudia Podio,
Eva Vanzella, Skira editore

Art director
Luigi Fiore

Copyediting
Francesca Bovetti

Layout
Antonio Carminati

Translations
Anna Knight

Photo Credits
© Courtesy of Moath Alofi

Published by

Museums Commission,
Ministry of Culture, Saudi Arabia
King Faisal Road, Al Bujairi,
Ad Diriyah 13711
Kingdom of Saudi Arabia

Skira editore spa
via Agnello, 18
20121 Milano
Italy
skira-arte.com

All rights reserved. No part of this
publication may be reproduced
or transmitted in any form or by
any means, electronic or mechanical,
including photography, recording
or any other information storage
and retrieval system, without prior
permission in writing from
the publisher

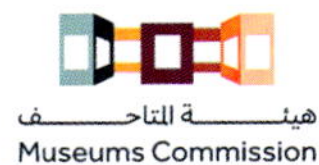

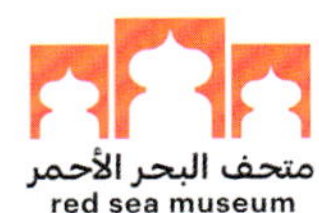

SKIRA

This book has been printed by
Galli Thierry Stampa Srl
on FSC®-certified paper

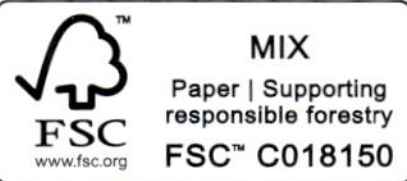

ISBN: 978-603-8481-14-1
(Ministry of Culture)
ISBN: 978-88-572-4890-5
(Skira editore)

Distributed in USA, Canada, Central
& South America by ARTBOOK | D.A.P
75 Broad Street Suite 630, New York,
NY 10004, USA
Distributed elsewhere in the world by
Thames and Hudson Ltd,
181A High Holborn, London
WC1V 7QX, United Kingdom